SUEÑOS

WORLD SPANISH

Tutor's Guide

Patrick Collins

BBC Books

Sueños: World Spanish course book, audio cassettes or CDs, Activity Book, Tutor's Guide and Tutor's cassette pack are linked to the content of the BBC TV and Radio language series **Sueños: World Spanish**.

TV and radio programmes first broadcast autumn 1995.

Television producer: Terry Doyle
Radio producer: Mick Webb
Audio producer: Colette Thomson
Developed by the BBC Language Unit

Tutor's Guide
Edited by Harriette Lanzer
Proofread by Janine Drake
Designed by Beatriz Custodio, for Book Creation
 Services, Ltd, London
Typeset by Gene Ferber, for Book Creation Services, Ltd,
 London
Illustrations and artwork by Beatriz Custodio and
 Sylvie Rabbe, for Book Creation Services, Ltd, London

ISBN 0 563 399287

Published by BBC Books, a division of BBC Worldwide Ltd
Woodlands, 80 Wood Lane, London W12 0TT
First published 1995

Printed and bound in Great Britain by
Ebenezer Baylis Ltd, Worcester

Covers printed by Clays Ltd, St Ives plc

Contents

Introduction

Components of a typical lesson

No two lessons are the same. However, there are a number of components which need to be considered in lesson planning. In order to be successful, a lesson generally has to be varied and interesting for the students and, at the same time, leave them with a sense of achievement.

There are general guidelines which will ensure this and what follows should be seen in that light. It would be a serious error to mistake it for a 'model' lesson to be copied at all times and in all circumstances. It is a set of guidelines for a sample lesson in which new language is introduced to the students and meaningful opportunities for practice given.

START OF LESSON: AIM

The beginning of the lesson needs to be clear and purposeful. It is necessary to explain, in simple terms, even in English, the aim of the lesson. This provides a clear context and helps the learners to make sense of new language, by enhancing their ability to guess the meanings and by giving them a set of clues to guide them.

REVISION

Before introducing the new language, there should be a brief warm-up of language which has already been covered and which will usefully contribute to the students' understanding of the new language. So, for example, if the students are being taught the time, it is important to revise the numbers thoroughly beforehand. If the new language relates to asking prices and paying, it might be useful to revise food and drink and numbers. Usually, the content of the lesson suggests what revision is most appropriate.

INPUT

New language should then be presented orally to the students in a gradual way, i.e. with an element of grading which is appropriate to the age and stage of the students. While input is going on, it is useful to spread questions around the classroom, so that all students can participate.

Errors should be handled sensitively so that students do not feel embarrassed about getting things wrong. A useful technique for correcting stubborn errors is to move from the student who is unable to produce the desired language, to a student who is more confident (preferably one sitting close to the student who made the original error) and, once a correct answer has been elicited, to return to the first student, so that he/she has a second opportunity to produce a correct answer.

FEEDBACK

After an oral presentation of the new language, it is useful to ask students if they have spotted the pattern/regularity and to confirm or reject their hypotheses. This is the point when explanations of grammatical points can help clarify and categorize the knowledge which the students have just gained about an aspect of the Spanish language.

CONSOLIDATION

Once the pattern has been established, the transfer from oral to written practice can take place. Students copy the model and, if necessary, the pattern can be highlighted once more, taking advantage of the visual support.

PRACTICE

This is the point where listening activities, group- or pairwork and written exercises are presented. They should all contain an appropriate element of grading.

PRODUCTION

It is important that there is a clear functional outcome to each new stage in language learning, which allows the students to combine the language they may already know with the language they have just learned. This encourages them to see that the language is real and can be used for getting things done, as well as giving them a sense of making progress.

END

The end of the lesson should be orderly and you should think about appropriate activities/exercises, within the capabilities of the students, which they might be asked to do in their own time and which will encourage them to maintain their interest in the language.

GENERAL

Two important overall considerations should be made. Firstly, as tutors, you must endeavour to use the target language as much as is possible and appropriate. Secondly, all four skills (listening, speaking, reading and writing) should be involved and combined in the lesson.

Stages of language learning

In order to achieve efficient learning, it is important for us to recognize the three main stages into which all language learning activity can be categorized:
- Input
- Practice
- Production.

By classifying activities according to the stage into which they best fit, you can identify which tasks are appropriate at any given point, and create a framework for judging the suitability of additional exercises and activities which you may wish to consider for inclusion in a lesson, or as part of an additional task for students.

Each chapter of this *Tutor's Guide* is structured following this pattern, so that you can easily identify the stage of learning which is being supported at any given point in the course. It is therefore important to recognize some of the kinds of activities which are involved at each stage and to describe how they should be approached in the classroom context.

INPUT

The input stage is the point at which the meaning of new language is made clear to the learners and they are given examples of appropriate use, which can form the basis of their own model of the language. This model will be key to their being able to manipulate the language properly for their own purposes and to develop successfully an appropriate model of the way in which Spanish conveys meanings.

Selection

If learning is to be efficient, then input in the foreign language needs to be prepared very carefully. For it is only by short-circuiting the natural learning process, by means of careful selection, sequencing and grading of language, that the learners can eventually reach similar levels of communicative competence to those of the native speaker.

The writers of **Sueños** have selected language which satisfies the criteria outlined above. It balances the need to provide examples of language which might be encountered in a 'natural' context of language use, with the need to select language which helps the learners to see the regularities of the language and thus help them to build their own model of how the language works. In practice, this means that, rather than simply selecting language on the basis of situations and/or functions, it is also necessary to take into consideration structural elements of the language.

Consequently, selection involves, on most occasions, choosing language that can be learned from, rather than simply learned, language that is plausible, rather than simply 'authentic', and language that has a high transfer value – i.e. can be used in many different contexts, rather than specific to one given context and/or time.

Sequencing

Young children learn their first language by a process of trial and error, which involves testing out hypotheses about how the language works. This process of hypothesis formulation, testing and adaptation is also present in many other facets of human learning. Through this process of discovery, which hypothesis formulation and testing involves, humans learn to make predictions about the behaviour and attitudes of others, and even about everyday events like the weather.

Therefore, the process of inputting new language needs to build on the learners' existing tendency to formulate and test hypotheses, to look for regularities and to establish 'the rule'. This will help to build confidence in learners about their own ability to deduce the rules and regularities of the language which they are learning.

This is particularly the case with students engaged in courses with a large self-access component. Unless they are encouraged to look for regularities in the foreign language and to build their own model of how the foreign language works, they are likely to engage in exercises which put a great deal of emphasis on memorizing unanalyzed chunks of language.

Given the limitations imposed by the impoverished context of the foreign language classroom, structural elements – the scaffolding of the language – need to be highlighted in order to improve the efficiency with which students formulate their hypotheses and to assist them in remembering newly-discovered structures in meaningful categories.

This does not mean spending time discussing structural elements of the target language in the learners' mother tongue, as the starting point for foreign language learning, as was previously the case in grammar-based approaches. Rather, it means trying to expose learners to language which has been carefully selected and sequenced. Then, by means of judicious graded presentations, they can be helped to develop their own model of how a given aspect of the Spanish language works.

After the input of the new language items in Spanish, it is necessary to ensure that the learners have correctly identified the regularities of the particular structure of the language, by confirming or rejecting their hypotheses.

GRADING

If learners are to feel comfortable about using the language, you need to introduce the new language gradually, beginning with simple forms and building up to the most complex. The most useful way to achieve this is through grading of questions which allow the learners to move from simple to complex statements by means of carefully planned steps.

It is important to recognize that such grading of input is not artificial. Nor is it exclusive to the foreign language learning context. Indeed, it is readily observable in the so-called 'caretaker speech' which takes place between adults and small children. Adults tend to adapt their use of language to suit the needs of the child, and if the meaning is not clear, they will elicit an appropriate response by asking a series of questions, which are themselves graded according to level of difficulty. As tutors, you too need to adapt your use of language in a similar way, to suit the needs of the learners.

Additionally, it is essential in language learning, as in all other areas of teaching, to give positive feedback and encouragement to the learners. Adult learners do not find it patronizing or inappropriate if their efforts are praised. Indeed they are more likely to feel encouraged to persevere when the going gets more difficult. **¡Eso es! ¡Bien! ¡Muy bien! ¡Excelente! ¡Perfecto!** or even **¡Fenomenal¡** can all be used for this purpose.

For the purposes of foreign language teaching, it is helpful to make use of five levels of grading. It is important to stress at this point that input at each of the five levels demands a certain degree of briskness and flexibility, if students are to derive benefit from the activity and are not to be left with a feeling of tedium.

In order to illustrate the different levels below, assume that the time is being taught, in particular, expressions for the hours on the clock.

1 Repetition
This level is important in allowing the students to become familiar with the pronunciation of Spanish and to have the opportunity to practise pronunciation. As with all levels, there are usually two stages: group followed by individual. Before each one, it is important to provide the students with a model answer to emulate.

a) In the first stage, the learners are given the opportunity to hear and repeat in a group. This provides a context which is protective of the individual and which allows students to practise making 'foreign' sounds in the anonymity of a group, without feeling embarrassed or intimidated.

b) The second stage involves repetition by individuals and it provides a useful opportunity to identify errors in pronunciation or in auditory perception at an early stage, when correction can prove considerably effective. In such a situation, it is important to move briskly around the class inviting students, or a sample of students, to repeat a given phrase or item of vocabulary.

2 True/False
The second level of grading involves the learners in identifying whether a particular auditory signal corresponds with a presented image or some other visual stimulant, such as an OHT or a video recording. This level of grading can be particularly useful in the initial phase of language learning, when learners are still becoming familiar with the new sounds of the language. Here, you could hold up a clockface depicting six o'clock and say, in an enquiring tone: **¿Son las siete? ¿Sí o no?** (**¿Verdad o falso?**)

3 Alternatives
The third level of grading involves the learners in selecting from a number of alternatives. So, using the example of time, hold up the clockface depicting three o'clock and ask: **¿Son las tres o son las cinco?** Then elicit the answer from students: **Son las tres.**

4 No + correct answer
The penultimate level of grading requires the learners to spot an incorrect statement and to correct it. At this point, hold up a clockface depicting four o'clock and, using a questioning tone, say to the students: **¿Son las seis?** This elicits the answer: **No, son las cuatro.**

5 Target question
The final level of grading presents the most difficult kind of question to the learners, who have no support in ascertaining the answer. Yet, curiously, it is frequently the first question which students face in the foreign language classroom. As its name suggests, the aim of the target question is to elicit the response which uses the newly-learned language in a totally unsupported manner.

Target questions are easily identifiable because they usually include one of the interrogative words: **¿Quién? ¿Qué? ¿Cuál? ¿Cuándo? ¿Dónde? ¿Por qué?** At this level, hold up a clockface depicting six o'clock and ask: **¿Qué hora es?** This elicits the answer: **Son las seis.**

The purpose of grading
These stages of grading not only provide a useful guide for levels of difficulty, in terms of input, but they also provide a helpful diagnostic matrix for identifying learners' errors and level of comprehension of given structures. Frequently, students may not be able to answer a target question, where they will be able to answer a question which offers alternative answers. Progress can be made by taking the students up through the levels of grading from the level at which they are able to answer confidently, to a level of greater independence.

All language can be graded using the above formula, though it is not always necessary to use every stage of the grading for all learners. The key guiding principles to be applied in deciding which levels of grading you need to use, will be the same as for other aspects of input, namely, what is appropriate to the age and stage of the learners?

As with grammar-based approaches, there exists the grave danger of turning this activity, from what is an essential tool of language teaching, into an instrument of drudgery by applying grading in a mechanical fashion. This can have disastrous consequences for teaching, not least because of the effect on learners' motivation as a result of the boredom they experience. It is therefore essential to consider the needs of the students and their level of understanding, when deciding which levels of grading are appropriate.

So, for example, with a group of students who have been studying Spanish for one term and who are familiar with the graded approach, it might be appropriate to move directly from the repetition level to the alternatives level and from there straight to using target questions, ignoring the intermediate stages. This is something which the you must decide in the light of your knowledge of the students.

PROVIDING MEANINGFUL CONTEXT

If the skills of hypothesis formulation and testing are to be further developed and utilized in the foreign language classroom, support for meaning needs to be provided. The provision of a meaningful context which helps clarify the meaning of the spoken or written language enables the learners and you to avoid over-reliance on the mother tongue.

Rich contextual clues to meaning cannot therefore be regarded as simply an optional component of any language course, but must be an indispensable component of good practice in the foreign language classroom. Moreover, if the contextual clues which you provide for the students are supportive of meaning, it will help to avoid the need for the use of complex grammatical terminology, which, in the initial stages of language learning, at least, only make difficult concepts even more abstract.

In the initial stages, contextual support for learning will inevitably be visual: flashcards, realia, OHTs, etc. However, as the learners progress, language which is already known will come to form part of the context for meaning of new language. If the learners know the months of the year, for example, then it will be possible to teach them the seasons through the medium of the target language, by describing the seasons in terms of the months of the year, and the weather, for example, in terms of the seasons.

This is an important principle of language teaching which helps to maximize use of the target language. That is to say, after the initial stages of language learning, the target language provides its own context, and new language items and structures can be explained in terms of known items and structures.

PAIR- AND GROUPWORK

Pairwork has a number of important advantages in the foreign language classroom, which are worth enumerating. In the first place, it allows for maximum use of the target language. Students can usually practise listening, reading and writing at home, but they have little opportunity to speak the language. Pairwork gives the opportunity for additional practice.

Pairwork reduces the anxiety level for those students who are shy about 'performing' in front of the class. Moreover, students tend to react better to correction by their peers in a small group than they do to public correction by their tutor.

Pair- and groupwork allow for variation in the pace of the lesson and thus obviate boredom and maintain interest.

Finally, pairwork allows us to move away from 'front stage' and circulate among the students to monitor and correct or help those students who are having difficulty.

But, of course, in order to be successful, pairwork needs to be set up properly, beginning with the recognition that it is a follow-up or practice activity and not an activity for presenting new language. It allows students to practise language that has been newly presented and, sometimes, to extend it.

The stage at which pairwork is appropriate is important because most of the problems which stem from pairwork are the result of insufficient preparation of the language that students require to accomplish the set task. This leads to a whole series of problems, the most common of which are error practice (students have not had sufficient opportunity to hear the language before engaging in pairwork and so produce incorrect variations) and so-called 'TV talk' (students have failed to understand the activity, often because their tutor has failed to explain clearly what is requried, and so they resort to talking about what they saw on TV the previous night).

Suitable activities for pairwork

a) Using some of the levels of grading, students take turns asking each other questions, perhaps based on a grid on an OHT. This need not last more than a few minutes and requires no written work.

b) Dialogues – new language can be embedded in a dialogue and students can practise graded activities based on it. This provides a useful transition to reading and writing, in which the students match sound and the written form aloud.

Dialogues can be graded, beginning with students simply reading aloud, before doing substitution activities and then moving on to free dialogues.

c) Role plays – these involve more open use of new structures or patterns in scenes. They can have instructions/guidance for the students in writing, in English or in symbols.

d) Information-gap – these involve activities in which the students are required, by using the target language, to discover information which their partner has, at the same time as passing on, to their partner, information which they have and their partner does not. It can also include comparison of pictures, or finding out information about their partner's likes and dislikes and other such mini-surveys.

The main features of these activities are that they involve a more meaningful context for the new language, can be graded to suit the level of the student and can involve more than simply listening or speaking. Once students have completed the task, it is important to get feedback by inviting some of them to demonstrate for the rest of the class what they have just practised.

Avoiding problems

In conducting pairwork, problems can be avoided or minimized by observing the following guidelines:

a) Build up gradually the amount of time which students are involved in pairwork.

b) Give clear instructions and a demonstration, where necessary.

c) Circulate and monitor the students' performance.

d) Ensure feedback at the end, i.e. a performance by the students or correction of an information-gap activity.

e) Provide students with a talkcard or worksheet to focus their attention and keep them working 'on task'.

WORKSHEETS

Practice activities can be provided by means other than pair- and groupwork. But, in order to be successful, they need to satisfy a number of criteria. Firstly, there must be a clear purpose to them, i.e. one which identifies particular structures/lexical sets which students are required to recognize or manipulate. Secondly, it is important to be clear about the prior knowledge of the language which you assume the students to have. Thirdly, you need to draw a clear distinction between teaching, in which students are assisted in learning new language, and testing, where you are interested in finding out what the students know.

It is perhaps worth underlining this point, for it is one which is a source of difficulties in the foreign language classroom. The purpose of testing is to measure how much and how well students have learned (and indeed you have taught) new language. Do not believe that, by means of testing, students are going to make a great deal of progress. Indeed, as is known from other aspects of human development, human beings do not grow taller by virtue of being measured. The only valid purpose of testing in the classroom is diagnostic.

ORDER OF SKILLS

The usual order in which skills are practised is aural to oral, and reading to writing. A good, general rule is that beginner students should not be required to say what they have not heard, to read what they have not said, or to write what they have not read.

Aural

Students listen to a series of short conversations/dialogues and tick a chart or fill a grid with appropriate symbols to show they have correctly identified the spoken word. This grid can form the basis of a whole series of activities including pairwork and writing, to give further, mixed-skill practice in the new language.

Oral

As previously discussed, pair- and groupwork are particularly useful as a means of giving practice. Students can practise asking and answering questions on a grid which depicts fruits, or on a train timetable or they could base their discussion on a picture of, say, the interior of a house, or on a diagram. An information-gap paircard can also form the basis of the activity.

Reading/Writing

It is not without reason that reading has been labelled the 'forgotten third skill'. Yet a great variety of activities can be devised to give suitable practice in this skill, both on its own and in conjunction with other skills. Using grids derived from initial oral practice, a whole series of graded exercises can be done, beginning with recognition activities where the students match words/phrases with pictures, trace directions based on written instructions, join two parts of a sentence, answer true or false questions, or select the correct answer in a multiple-choice activity.

They can then move on to comprehension activities involving answering questions based on signs, letters, short written dialogues, letters, short articles, etc.

Finally, they can engage in reading activities which require skimming short passages for gist or scanning for specific information. These activities do not require a complex text, but can be used from the earliest stages using simple dialogues.

Writing

As with other skills, learning to write in the foreign language needs to be staged. Activities need to move from purely reproductive activities, involving copying and using model answers, through less reproductive stages where students have to select from alternative answers and correct wrong answers, to productive activities which require students to answer target questions and compose their own texts by, for example, making up dialogues, writing letters and writing descriptions.

Unidad 5 *En el mercado*
Teaching with Sueños World Spanish: a framework lesson

The purpose of this section of the *Tutor's Guide* is to familiarize you with the course book's approach and to offer suggestions on how to handle the material successfully. It aims to serve as a reference for working through all other units.

There are a number of elements which a lesson needs in order to be successful: variety, interest, structure and, most importantly for the students, it must leave them with a sense of achievement.

No two lessons are the same and there is no such thing as a model lesson. What follows is a sample of what can be done with a group of adult learners, using unit 5. Other units do not contain the same level of detailed guidance, but they do contain some specific suggestions and photocopiable materials.

Functions

- Shopping for groceries
- Shopping for fruit and vegetables
- Finding out what things cost

Grammar

- Present tense: **querer**
- Demonstrative adjectives
- Question words: **¿cuánto/a/os/as?**

Vocabulary

- Food
- Shops

Revision

- Quantities and numbers

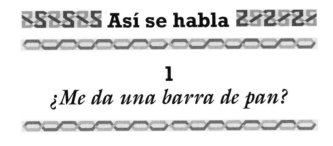

Así se habla

1
¿Me da una barra de pan?

Start of lesson

Aim

So that students can see, from the outset, what new language they will be learning, you need to explain, in simple terms or in English, the aim of the lesson. This is done at the beginning of each unit and is implicit in each exercise.

It is worthwhile reading the objectives with the students and reviewing what is in the unit and why and in what circumstances this language can be useful: 'Shopping for groceries is an extremely important skill to learn in any language. But the new language that we learn will also be useful in other areas of living in a Spanish-speaking country, such as cooking, going to restaurants/cafés or any area where we need to talk about quantities and measurements.'

It is also worthwhile making the new learning point of each activity explicit: 'In this activity you are going to learn the names of groceries and how to ask for them in a shop.'

Revision

Before introducing new language, you need to revise language which the students have already covered and which reappears in the new setting. Since the new language relates to asking for quantities, prices and paying for shopping, it is useful to revise numbers, food and drink, places in town and **(no) hay**. Usually, the content of the lesson suggests what revision is most appropriate.

1

Input

The new language needs first to be presented aurally to the students in a graded manner. The first stage of this input is provided in Activity 1, accompanied by the recording. It is important to explain to students that listening, like all other skills, needs practice. Otherwise, they can easily become demoralized when they don't understand spoken language on the first hearing.

Ask students to look at Activity 1 while you play the recording. Following the guidance given in the course book, students match up the sounds they hear with the illustrations in the book.

You will have to keep stopping the recording, establishing the link between what is heard and the illustrations and going back to listen again. This is best done on a machine with a counter, which you use to mark the point at which a new item starts, so that it can be easily found again to review the answers.

When students have had an opportunity to listen several times, you can use OHT/Flashcards 5.1 together with a series of graded questions to give practice in speaking. If you are using the flashcards, draw an outline of a shop front on the board and attach the flashcards in a suitable position.

Introduce the groceries by pointing to a flashcard and asking, for example: **¿En la tienda de comestibles hay leche? ¿Sí o no?** When you want students to answer **no**, remove the food in question. Do this with all the foods several times and at a brisk pace.

Once this has been done, move to the next level and, after removing one of the two foods, ask alternative questions: **En la tienda de comestibles ¿hay patatas fritas o hay galletas?** Elicit the answer: **Hay galletas.** Do this with all the foods, several times, varying the food that is pointed to and the alternatives that are offered.

Next, remove one of the foods, for example **las galletas** and point at **los huevos,** saying in an assertive tone: **Hay galletas en la tienda de comestibles.** Look again at the shop front and correct your error, by announcing: **No. Hay huevos.** Repeat this tactic for all the foods, several times, chorally at first and then individually.

Finally, point at an item of food (for example, **el jamón**) and ask: **¿Qué hay en la tienda de comestibles?** to elicit the response: **Hay jamón.**

Note: Errors should be handled sensitively, so that students do not feel embarrassed about getting things wrong.

Feedback

After practising new language orally/aurally, revise the concept of gender in Spanish and how it differs from English. This does not need to be done using technical language – talking about **el** and **la** words can be appropriate for some students. Linking up **el** words with **un/los** words, and **la** words with **una/las** words can help clarify and consolidate students' conceptual knowledge of gender in Spanish.

Note: While the input is going on, try to ensure that all students participate, and give lots of encouraging praise.

Consolidation

Once you have established the pattern, the transfer from aural/oral to written practice can take place. Students copy a model sentence in writing: **En la tienda de comestibles hay leche.** This is an important step towards written production and many errors will occur in copying. Use these as an opportunity to focus students' attention on the details of spelling. This provides an ideal opportunity to revise the Spanish alphabet, by asking: **¿Cómo se escribe...?**

Input

New language which is now input in context is: **¿Qué más? ¿Algo más? Nada más.**

2

When the basic vocabulary has been inputted, you can turn to hearing it used in context. This is done by moving on to Activity 2. Play the recording through several times, using a grid, like the one here, to help students identify the groceries.

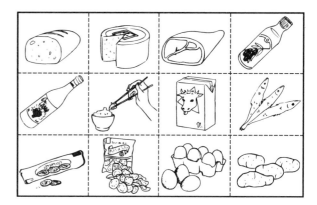

Begoña
Ion

In correcting the exercise, you can ask a range of graded questions to give further practice in using the structures which have just been learned.

Note: Correction should never simply be a question of right or wrong, or of counting marks, but it is a valuable opportunity to give further practice of new language.

Así se acostumbra

Practice/Pairwork

Students can now use their grid from Activity 2 for a short practice using the vocabulary and structures they have just learned, by taking it in turns to be the shop assistant and the customers, Ion and Begoña. This gives additional, useful practice of the expressions: **¿Qué más? ¿Algo más? Nada más.**

Now that students are familiar with the basic groceries and key structures they might encounter in the context of shopping, it is time to introduce a range of ways of asking for groceries (or anything else).

3

Play the recording. It is a good idea for students to listen first without reading from the book, so that they get into the habit of listening for and recognizing language they have already encountered. Once more, you should play the recording through several times, and in stages, to allow the students time to absorb the new language.

Así se dice

Explore, with the aid of English, the new structures and their appropriate use in *Así se dice*. Students will want explanations for the differences between **quiero...,** **quería...** and **quisiera...** which you should explain in terms of levels of formality and elicit the means by which this is achieved in English.

Note: It is important to make comparisons with English every now and then, as this can be a useful point of reference for students. As Tolstoy said, 'one can never know one's own language properly until one has learned someone else's language.'

4 Y ahora tú

The range of expressions for making requests can be further consolidated here where students work in pairs, or in groups, on designing questions to ask for the groceries listed. In order to consolidate the activity, it is helpful to get students to write down their suggestions of ways of asking. This can be supplemented by doing Worksheet 5.2 where students practise using the different ways of asking for things in the shop.

While students are engaged in the activity, take advantage to circulate, monitor their performance and assist those who are having problems. At the end, it is useful to get a couple of pairs to 'perform' the pairwork for the rest of the group and to make sure that everyone has followed the activity.

This can be followed by an aural comprehension exercise in which you read a number of food items from a list of shopping and students have to tick them off in the blank row at the bottom of the grid.

5

By carefully graded stages, the students have been introduced to groceries and ways of asking for items. In order to be able to function more efficiently as shoppers in a Spanish-speaking country, they need to specify quantities of each product. The aim of Activity 5 is to give them the language for this.

Presentation/Input
Before the students tackle Activity 5, it is necessary to familiarize them with common weights, measures and containers for food and drink. This can be done using OHT/Flashcards 5.3. Using a graded presentation of these items, you can input them. The stages of presentation are as follows:

Repetition: Point to each flashcard in turn and give the Spanish expression. Invite the students to repeat, at first in a group and then individually: **Es un litro. Es kilo y medio...**

True/False: Make a statement about each container/measure and invite the students to identify whether it is correct or not, by answering **sí** or **no: ¿Es un litro – sí o no?**

Alternatives: Point to a measure/weight and give alternative answers, only one of which is correct: (pointing to **litro y medio**) **¿Es un litro o es litro y medio?**

Correction: Point to **100 gramos** and ask: **¿Es un litro?** Elicit the answer: **No. Son 100 gramos.**

Target question: Point to weight/measure and ask: **¿Qué medida es?** Elicit the answer: **Es medio kilo.**

This whole procedure need not take more than five minutes. You can then move on to containers and follow the same pattern.

Practice
Before students can tackle Activity 5, which tests their recognition of weights, measures and containers, they need to get some more controlled practice using the new language. This could be done by doing the pairwork activity on Worksheet 5.4.

Production/Role play
It is important that there should be a clear functional outcome to each new stage of language learning, which allows the students to combine the language they may already know with the language they have just learned. This encourages them to see that the language is real and can be used for getting things done, as well as giving them a sense of making progress – the following two activities do just that.

6

This activity should be seen as a rehearsal of the core element of the role play. It should therefore be done, individually or in pairs, by the students and answers revised with the class as a whole, before moving on to Activity 7.

7 Y ahora tú

Having practised the language needed to shop for food and drink, students can now work together in groups to prepare role plays of the shopping for the picnic ingredients. The language needed to build these role plays can be obtained from earlier ones involving Ion and Begoña. Students should be encouraged to make the role play as elaborate as possible and to include as much language as possible from previous lessons. This should include greetings, asking names, where people live, occupations, etc. It might also involve some of the produce which is requested not being available and alternatives having to be suggested.

8 De tiendas
Revision
You can introduce the names of shops. It is worth pointing out to students that, while the tendency for small shops to disappear and be replaced by supermarkets exists in Spanish-speaking countries, as elsewhere, supermarket departments are still called by the names of the small shops. Revise the names of groceries using OHT/Flashcards 5.1 before getting students to do the matching exercise in Activity 8. Before moving on to use the new vocabulary, students will need more practice using the names of shops. This can be done using Worksheet 5.5.

9

Play the recording and get the students to write down the name of the shop where the Spanish woman does her shopping. (You will need to assume that students can guess what **el mercado** is – it is explained later in the unit.)

10

Read over this activity with the students and get them to do the exercise. Tell them that the products referred to are in the rectangle to the right of the text.

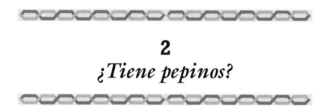

2
¿Tiene pepinos?

1

Input

Students need to learn the names of common fruits and vegetables, and to consolidate their knowledge of the plural forms. Categorize the range of fruits and vegetables to make the learning easier. This is done in Activity 1, where cognates have been isolated. Before reading the exercise, it is useful for the students to hear the new language, so read the words out and encourage them to say the English equivalents, before they look at their books. Otherwise, English pronunciation might interfere with the Spanish. The matching exercise can then safely be done following the instructions in the course book.

A similar procedure is needed for the other vegetables and fruits. Using graded presentation, introduce the new items. You may find it helpful to divide the language as follows: **manzanas, naranjas, almendras, cebollas, zanahorias, lechugas; mangos, plátanos, pimientos, pepinos, ajos.**

The presentation can be based on the fruit and vegetables on OHT/Flashcards 5.6. Uncover one at a time, in the order set out above, beginning with the feminine nouns, before moving on to the masculine nouns. Go through whatever stages you think are appropriate for your students. The stages in order of difficulty, from easiest to most difficult are:

1 Pointing to the OHT, you emphasize the latter half of the statement and say: **En el puesto, hay manzanas.** Students repeat: **Hay manzanas.** This is then repeated for the remaining items.

2 **En el puesto de Juan hay manzanas. ¿Sí o no?**

3 **¿En el puesto de Berta hay naranjas o peras?**

4 **En el puesto de Marta hay almendras.** This is a

false statement so students must supply the correct item: **No, hay… .**

5 **¿Qué fruta hay en el puesto de Tulio?**

Whatever the case, the input needs to be done using all the fruits several times and at a brisk pace, so that students get a reasonable opportunity to practise them, but do not suffer from boredom. No more than ten minutes should be spent on the input.

Take advantage to extend the students' range of language by asking other, related target questions: **¿Qué otra fruta hay en el puesto?** and when the students answer correctly, follow up with: **¿Qué más?**

2

Consolidation

Students can now listen to the recording and complete the ticking activity. As with all listening exercises, students need more than one opportunity to hear the speaker, so you need to keep stopping the recording and going back.

When the exercise is completed, confirm what each fruit is in English and elicit information about genders. Highlight the differences in pronunciation, particularly in respect of **melón** and **limón** and other cognates. It is worth pointing out that words which end in **on** in Spanish tend to have the accent on the last syllable. Read *Así se acostumbra* so that students are familiar with the concept and importance of **el mercado** in the Hispanic world.

Practice/Pairwork

Play the recording. Get the students to tick off the fruits, in pencil, on the picture. Remember, students need to hear the recording several times and you will have to stop the tape frequently. If they seem to be having too much difficulty, offer them alternatives yourself from which to choose. The information can be transferred to Worksheet 5.7 which introduces several market sellers and lists the produce they sell. Students take it in turns to find out who sells what. In doing this activity, students can practise asking a range of questions: **¿Qué fruta vende Paco? ¿Quién vende mangos? ¿Marta vende plátanos. Sí o no?**

This gives good practice in asking questions and practising vocabulary for produce, which students will need in the next stage when they come to asking about quantities and prices.

3

Now that students are familiar with the names of produce, you can introduce weights together with three ways of asking for things. This should not present problems, since students have encountered these elements earlier in the unit. However, you will still have to take care to stop the recording and repeat it several times, to build students' confidence. When you are correcting the activity, it is worth highlighting the new structures in *Así se dice*.

4

You can now further consolidate the new language by doing this listening activity. You could build in support for it by using a tick chart like the one below and asking: **¿Qué compra Carmen? ¿Cuánto compra? ¿Cuánto es?**

	kg	precio
pimiento verde		
pimiento rojo		
pimiento amarillo		
tomates		
cebollas		
pepinos		

5 *Y ahora tú*

Production

Now that students have practised the new language thoroughly, they can move on to activities which require them to use it in a realistic way, by making up dialogues. Encourage them to elaborate their responses, by specifying a minimum number of items which should be included in the list. Students can then use the grid from the previous activity to help them with weights.

Once more, as with all productive activities, you should encourage students to incorporate as much other language into their role plays as possible. When students have had a reasonable amount of time to work on this activity (between five and ten minutes) encourage a few pairs to perform their dialogue for the rest of the group.

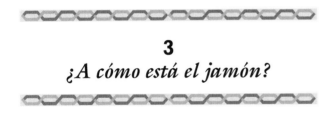

3
¿A cómo está el jamón?

Revise some numbers, using some of the activities which students are already familiar with in this context. Start with 1–20. Then do tens to 100, then 100s to 1,000 and finally 1,000s to 20,000. Among the practice activities include some calculations which require the use of high numbers.

Put a few flashcards of produce on the board and write some prices below them. Begin by pointing out the price of the tomatoes, for example, and saying: **Los tomates están a doscientos el kilo.** Invite students to repeat this and the prices of the other items on the stall, first chorally and then individually.

Now introduce other levels of grading, according to the needs of the learners. The kind of questions are on the following scale: **¿Los tomates están a trescientos el kilo? ¿Sí o no? ¿Los tomates están a trescientos el kilo o a cuatrocientos el kilo? ¿Los tomates están a cien el kilo?** (Eliciting the response: **No, están a trescientos el kilo.**) And finally, you can ask the target question: **¿A cómo están los tomates?**

1

Input

Play the recording several times. In correcting the exercise, concentrate on the price of the goods.

> ### *Así se dice*

In looking at this, you need to highlight differences between singular and plural forms of the verb. You may also be asked about the difference between **está/es** and **están/son**.

Avoid the temptation to explain all the differences between **ser** and **estar**. Limit explanations to the fact that **está** and **están** tend to refer to **ahora** or **hoy**, whereas **es** and **son** are more permanent. The extent of the explanation depends, of course, on the age and stage of the learners. Understanding the differences is something which happens over a period of time, through exposure, rather than instantly through a one-off 'golden rule'.

2

Practice

Students need to practise asking for prices and this can be done using the information provided in the short lists in the central column of page 54 in the course book. This activity should be done in pairs. Encourage students to write down their answers, so that, when the exercise is being corrected, they can take turns to perform a short role play.

3

Listening practice

This listening activity has built-in support for the learner, in the form of prices already written down. The task is to match the recording with the prices as they appear in writing. As with all matching activities, predicting skills play an important role. Encourage the students to try to work out, in advance, what each price is likely to sound like in Spanish. Then, play the recording several times, stopping after each price is mentioned and going back to listen again. When this has been accomplished, play the recording through one final time, stopping to correct the exercise.

Note: It is important to get feedback from students about regularities they have noticed in the language –

how to ask prices, for example. This should then be confirmed by you, using *Así se dice*.

4

Practice

Finally, to ensure more opportunities for practice of numbers and prices, get students to do Activity 4. Check the total cost of the bill for the items asked for in Activity 2. Note that when doing the correction for this, or indeed any, exercise, try to use the opportunity to give more practice in Spanish. Copy the details of the bill on the board and get the students to provide answers in Spanish.

Las divisas

To help students learn the currencies and their countries of origin, you could combine this new language with known language. Read out the details below and ask the students to write them down. You can develop the exercise as far as you wish by adding in more examples of your own.

¿Dónde está?			
Nombre	Marco Antonio	María Florencia	Antonia Sánchez
Ciudad	Salamanca	Lima	Valparaíso
Tienda	frutería	charcutería	pastelería
Compra	manzanas/sandía	jamón/queso	dos pasteles de chocolate
Total	385 pesetas	2,000 sol oros	15,000 pesos
País			

This is a good opportunity to ask for other question words that students know, such as: **¿Cómo? ¿Dónde?** and to elicit meanings and a few examples of use. This can be done in Spanish, by asking simple questions, such as: **¿Qué otra pregunta se puede hacer?**

Production

This can be followed by a role play in which the students compose a simulation of a shopping trip to a market/shop for food.

▲▲▲▲▲▲ Temas ▲▲▲▲▲▲
El encuentro de los gustos

The *Temas* section in each unit will be of great interest to many of the students, who are interested not simply in learning the language, but also in gaining access to the vast culture which lies behind it. It is therefore extremely important to encourage this interest by exploring cultural issues, since by so doing you can enhance motivation.

Temas is divided into three sections. The first section looks at an issue of wider cultural significance. The second looks at an everyday aspect of Hispanic culture and the third section looks at an example of the literature which exists in Spanish.

El encuentro de los gustos

After reading through the passage on the Latin American origins with the students and the contents of the large variety of foods and drinks, which are now taken for granted, you could give them the following **¿Verdad o mentira?** statements on it. Remember, however, that this activity should not be treated very seriously and that a sense of humour is needed so that students do not feel they are being patronized.

1 The Conquistadores brought the tomato to the Aztecs, who called it the **jitomate**.
2 Corn was the staple diet of the Aztecs.
3 The Incas introduced the potato to the Conquistadores.
4 The Incas lived in the area that we now call Peru.
5 The pineapple has two different names in Spanish.
6 There is more than one variety of hot pepper.
7 **Tortillas** are made from maize, bananas, potato and Chile.
8 Red wine from Spain was added to the local drink in Mexico to make tequila.
9 **La chicha**, the Peruvian drink, is made from corn.
10 Latin American food and drink has remained free from outside influence.

Recetas de cocina

Work on the recipes can provide useful practice in using a dictionary and is the kind of activity which students can be asked to prepare at home. The activity can then be corrected briefly at the beginning of the next lesson.

"Oda a la cebolla"

The use of authentic literature is very motivating for students. Read the poem to them. Do not get bogged down in complex explanations of the use of the preterite tense in **hizo**. Just give the students the meaning and tell them they will come to it later on in the course.

There are numerous activities which can be based on the poem, once comprehension activities have been completed. Start with students finding the Spanish equivalents of phrases as indicated in the book. Then do this short exercise on matching up definitions.

1 tierra	a) grupo de planetas
2 cebolla	b) una flor bonita
3 planeta	c) no tiene dinero
4 constelación	d) una verdura redonda
5 rosa	e) el lugar donde vivo
6 agua	f) el sol es un...

7 mesa   g) el sitio donde como

8 pobre   h) líquido transparente

Reading

Reading, especially poetry, provides very good practice in pronunciation. Get the students to work in pairs, or in groups, preparing a reading of the poem. They could divide the poem into two or three sections and take turns at reading it, before presenting their final delivery to the class. This is good fun and very motivating.

✕✕◈ Veamos de nuevo ◈✕✕
Gramática

Before moving on to the next unit, it is worth reviewing what has been learned in this one and consolidating it. This can be done by going through *Veamos de nuevo* at a fairly brisk pace, since it is familiar territory.

▪ Un paso más

1 El mercado

This activity offers extension material for the students to tackle at their own pace. Filling in information from reading the passage is the first stage in the activity. Correct the exercise orally and practise different kinds of questions as well as revising much of the new vocabulary and structures which have been learned in this unit.

2 At work

Production

This activity is an extended role play in which the students play the role of a buyer in an import company. Encourage them to experiment and to incorporate as much 'other' language as they can. The final outcome should be a demonstration for the rest of the group, as this will give a clear functional aim to the activity.

3 Los menus de Arguiñano

More practice is given here in recognizing quantities. This should be corrected in class and you should take advantage to go over questions related to asking about amounts and quantities.

4 Checklist

The checklist is very useful for enabling students to gain a sense of achievement. It is worthwhile being fairly systematic about this. Go through briefly what is meant by each category and get the students to give you examples. You may be surprised how difficult it can be for students to categorize their learning in this way and how pleased they are when they realize just how much they can actually do. Reinforcing this sense of achievement enhances the students' self-esteem and, therefore, motivation.

Unidad 0 *¡Bienvenido al español!*

Functions

- Words that walk
- Saying hello and goodbye

Vocabulary

- Familiar words
- Greetings

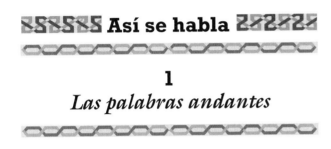

Así se habla

1
Las palabras andantes

1

Input

In order to give students the confidence to tackle learning Spanish, it is important to stress that they are not starting from zero but that they already have a great deal of knowledge about how language in general works, which they will be able to use. They are also familiar with a great many Spanish words which have either become part of English or are part of internationally-recognized expressions.

Read the words to the class, stopping after each one to encourage the group, as a whole, to pronounce the words. When this has been done, read them once more, without interruption and allow the students to listen and repeat without correction.

> *Así se acostumbra*

Read over this section which deals with more examples of the international dimension of the Spanish language. It might be helpful to refer to a map of the world, since many of the students may not know where some of the places mentioned actually are.

2

Practice

This gives the students the opportunity to follow up on the theme of familiar language, by matching up words or names which they have probably already encountered with explanations of their meaning.

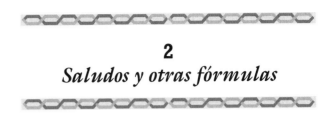

2
Saludos y otras fórmulas

1 *Saying hello*

Input/Listening

It is always a good idea to teach the students the simple greeting: **¡Hola!** Go around the class greeting students individually and then encourage them to greet you and each other.

When you have done this and students are reasonably confident about saying **¡Hola!** to each other, explain the many uses of the greeting. Write it on the board/ OHP and elicit from students the fact that **h** is not pronounced in Spanish.

Before playing the recording of the variety of ways of saying hello, read over the brief introduction in the book and elicit from students examples of different ways of saying the same thing in English. It is important to stop the recording after each greeting to give the students an opportunity to practise, first in chorus and then individually.

> *Así se dice*

Read over the outline of the different greetings and then give students the opportunity to practise them in pairs.

2

Production

Students read through the different scenarios and work out which greeting is most appropriate. In correcting this, elicit from the students the key information which indicates the most appropriate greeting.

3

Listening

Play the recording of the conversation between two people greeting each other. Students could be expected to guess the meaning of **fatal** and from there to deduce the meaning of **muy bien**.

Así se dice

The spectrum of possible replies to the question ¿Qué tal? is provided here. Give students additional practice using the paircards on Worksheet 0.1 in which they take it in turns to initiate and reply to the greeting.

Así se acostumbra

It is useful to introduce the concept of two different words for 'you' in Spanish. This, however, does not need to be elaborated on further at this stage, since full comprehension of the uses of usted and tú will come with time and exposure to more examples of actual use. Do not neglect to mention vos, as an alternative in Latin American countries.

4

Listening practice

Play the recording, one conversation at a time, taking time to repeat each section where necessary to enable the students to hear the important linguistic clues. When all the examples have been dealt with in this way, play the entire recording through once more, without pausing and then correct the activity. Here again, it is not simply a matter of deciding whether the students have arrived at the correct answer. You should take advantage of the opportunity to play the recording through once more, and correct in Spanish, giving encouragement, such as muy bien when students provide the correct answer.

5 Saying goodbye

Input

As with examples of ways of saying hello, you can now introduce ways of saying goodbye in Spanish.

Así se dice

Read over the variety of expressions for saying goodbye and highlight the need for the appropriate expression to be used, both in terms of the time of day and of the relationship with the person being addressed.

6 Y ahora tú

Production

Students need to supply one side of a conversation, in reply to greetings from another person. This should be done in stages to allow students to absorb the new language, and the rules for its use, with ease.

▲▲▲▲▲ Temas ▲▲▲▲▲

Gracias, muy amable

Saying please and thank you

Read over with the class the outline of the ways of saying please and thank you and the appropriate use of the expressions given.

Saying sorry/Excusing yourself

Once again, read over the range of expressions in Spanish for saying sorry or excusing yourself. It is necessary to reassure the students that they should not expect to learn all of these expressions at once. Rather, as they progress through the book, they will encounter these expressions again and they should recognize them. Only after meeting the expressions several times will they feel totally confident about using all of them.

✕✕ Veamos de nuevo ✕✕

▪ Práctica

A Hello and goodbye

Students should work first on their own on this activity. When they have decided which expressions are appropriate, they could work with a partner at preparing a mini-dialogue, which they subsequently perform for the rest of the class.

B The right expression

As an initial practice exercise in the use of the new expressions which they have just learned, students should work in pairs deciding which phrases to use in each of the situations outlined in the course book.

Unidad 1 *Primeras impresiones*

Functions

- Asking someone's name and giving yours
- Saying where you are from and where you live
- Saying what languages you speak

Grammar

- Present tense: **hablar, vivir, ser**
- Questions and question words: **¿Qué? ¿Cuál? ¿Dónde? ¿Cómo?**

Vocabulary

- Alphabet
- Countries
- Languages

Así se habla

1
¿Cómo te llamas?

1

Listening practice

Play the recording several times, to give students a good opportunity to hear the new sounds, before getting them to repeat the dialogues. When this has been done, go around the class asking students one of the three question forms, to establish that all three ways of asking someone's name are equally valid.

Así se acostumbra

Read over this section with students and explain the system of working out surnames. To reinforce the point, you could get students to imagine that the same system operated in English and ask them to work out what their surnames would be – you may be surprised at how many students do not know their mother's maiden name!

Así se dice

Get students to ask each other their names and to use the Spanish configuration when answering the question, for example: **Me llamo Jane Smith-Connelly.**

Move on to looking at the box and confirming the main ways in which the question can be put. Explain that the use of **¿Cómo te llamas? ¿Cómo se llama?** is more common in Spain, while **¿Cuál es tu/ su nombre?** is used more in Latin America.

Establish what is meant by 'formally' and give some guidance for the use of **usted**.

2

Practice

Get students to take it in turns to be the characters in the pictures and use this as an opportunity to set up a role play which you monitor by circulating to hear each pair. After a few minutes, get some of the students to 'perform' the role play.

3 *Y ahora tú*

Students get together in groups of about four or five and take it in turns to ask every member of the group his/her name.

4 *Nombres y apellidos*

Practice

When students have separated first names and surnames, do the correction on a grid on the board/OHP and take advantage of the opportunity to get students to practise pronunciation, by repeating the question: **¿Cómo se llama?**

5

Listening practice

Keep the *nombres y apellidos* grid in view of the students and play the recording. Once more, take advantage of the correction of the exercise to give more practice in asking and answering questions.

6 *El alfabeto español*

Input

It is worth taking time now to practise the Spanish alphabet using the recording of Spanish names.

When the recording has been played over several times and students have had an opportunity to repeat the names, first chorally and then individually, read through and elaborate on the guidelines given under pronunciation.

7

Pronunciation practice

Do this activity, by getting the students first of all to prepare the pronunciation of the Spanish surnames. Highlight the particular features of pronunciation in each word: **ll** in **Guillermo**, **rr** in **Carreras**, etc.

8

Listening practice

When playing the recording for the first time, encourage students not to look at the book. Explore the unknown language and encourage guessing about meaning. Get them to write down the name following the spelling given on the recording.

Now students can open the book and you can confirm their answers. Explain the difference between **nombre** and **apellido**.

> ### *Así se dice*

Consolidation

Highlight the use of the upside-down question mark in Spanish and the reason why it is needed, i.e. the only difference between a question and an affirmation in Spanish can be intonation. The upside-down question mark indicates to the reader that a question is about to be asked.

9 *Y ahora tú*

Production

This can be done as a pairwork activity. Students ask each other their names and how to spell them in Spanish. If they do not hear or understand what their partner says, students should begin to use **¿Cómo?** or **¿Repite, por favor?** to elicit repetition.

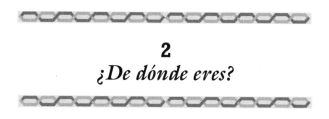

2
¿De dónde eres?

1 *Países de habla hispana*

Input

Explore the map of Spanish-speaking countries on OHT 1.1. Practise the names and correct any errors in pronunciation. You may wish to practise spelling by asking for the name of a country: **¿Cómo se llama este país? ¿Cómo se escribe el nombre de este país?** (pointing to the map)

Do an example first yourself, so that students have a model to copy.

2

Consolidation

Play the recording and get students to identify the missing countries and to spell them.

You can then move on to the information-gap pairwork based on semi-blank maps of Latin America on Worksheet 1.2. The student with map A needs to ask his/her partner with map B for the names of the countries missing on his/her map and vice versa.

3

Input

Play through the recording several times. On each occasion, try to elicit the possible meaning of each of the following: **Soy... ¿De dónde eres? Vivo en...** Draw attention to pronunciation, in particular **en**. Confirm or reject the students' hypotheses by referring to *Así se dice*.

> ### *Así se dice*

Consolidate the form of **ser** by reference to the paradigm of the singular form in the middle column.

Note: It is worth revising on a regular basis the 'words which can be used to ask questions' (interrogatives). Ask students for examples of questions which can be asked using these words and of possible answers. By now students have come across: **¿Cómo? ¿Cuál? ¿Dónde?**

4 *Y ahora tú*

Practice

Combine the questions so that, in groups of four or five, students take it in turns to ask the person on their right side three questions: **¿Cómo te llamas? ¿Dónde vives? ¿De dónde eres?** The student then turns to the rest of the group and says: **Se llama... Vive en... Es de...** In this way they work their way around the group.

Pairwork

Students can do the activity on Worksheet 1.3. They take it in turns to ask each other questions so that they can obtain the information missing on each of their cards.

Production

Ask students to write out sentences for each character. This will give good practice in transferring from speech to writing.

5

Listening practice

Play the recording and get students to fill in the grid with the missing details. You will still have to stop frequently and give students the opportunity to recapitulate on their answers.

This offers a good opportunity to revise the form of the third person singular.

6

Practice

Students write out full sentences. When the **origen** and **lugar de residencia** do not coincide, they can use **pero**. In addition to asking name and country, students can also ask: **¿Dónde vive?**

7 *Otros países*

Input

It is very important with these countries to insist on correct pronunciation of names which are so close to English. This can then be revised using flags, for example, as a prompt for the language/country/nationality.

The presentation takes the form of you giving the names of the countries and the students repeating them after you. This can be followed by a series of graded questions, including true/false statements; alternatives; wrong answers; student giving correct answer to target question: **¿Qué país es?**

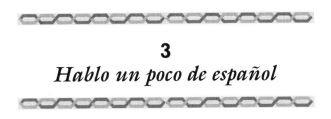

3
Hablo un poco de español

1 *Escuela de idiomas*

Input

After introducing this activity, ask some graded questions to ensure students are familiar with the languages. The illustrations in the book can serve the same purpose as flashcards with you pointing at the book to ask a series of graded questions.

2

Consolidation

Play the recording and get the students to identify the details of the interviewee as per instructions in the book.

3

Production

This activity provides a useful writing activity.

4 *Y ahora tú*

Practice

You can go round the class asking students what languages they speak. To make the activity more interesting, use the 'round-robin' pattern in which students take it in turn to ask: **¿Qué lenguas hablas?** They then listen to the answer and report back to the rest of the group using the third person singular form.

5

Listening practice

Useful listening practice can be provided by playing the recording and encouraging students to use the support offered by the grid.

6

Practice

Students can name the languages which the interviewees speak as a prelude to a more general revision of question forms.

When the activity has been done, use the completed grids in Activity 5 as the basis of pairwork, in which students ask each other questions about the information contained there. Once again, this is a good opportunity to rehearse interrogatives before doing the pairwork. The aim is for the students to ask as many questions as possible.

7 *Y ahora tú*

Practice

This can be done as before, using the 'round-robin' activity, or students can conduct a small survey within their group (six to eight is an ideal number on this occasion) to find out what languages are spoken, by taking turns to ask each other questions. Students should have to ask true/false or alternative questions first, before being allowed to ask target questions.

In order to assist students with this listening activity, it is useful to refer them back to *¿De dónde eres?* and use the map of Spanish-speaking countries as a tick chart.

Temas
El español: idioma mundial

Rather than simply reading through the *Temas* section, students could do the comprehension activities on Worksheet 1.4. The correction of answers will serve as the basis for a more focused and informed discussion of the issues raised.

✕✦ Veamos de nuevo ✦✕
Gramática

Now that students have had considerable exposure to the way in which Spanish uses verbal structure to convey the subject of an action, it is useful to summarize what they have discovered about the Spanish verb system. This is meaningful, because, through exposure to Spanish verbs, some students will have developed the concept of what a verb is.

At this stage, it is worth taking time to go over this ground to reinforce student understanding. This is done in the first section of *Veamos de nuevo*.

▪ *Práctica*

The exercises here are ideal for homework and can be corrected in class by you.

▪ *Un paso más*

Production

In order for students to retain their motivation, it is important for them to see that the language they have learned has a functional outcome. *Un paso más* provides such an outcome by giving the students meaningful and realistic tasks which require productive use of the language which has just been learned, by using more than one skill.

1 *Play your part!*

Encourage students to work on this activity on their own to begin with, so that they start to develop a measure of how much language they have retained that is now available for productive use.

When they have provided a first draft, it may be appropriate for them to compare outcomes with one or more other students, and to construct a role play around it. This allows each student to develop his/her own version.

2 *Gente de hoy*

Students read the passage to find relevant information to fill in the grid, as instructed. This develops and tests the important reading skill of scanning a longer passage for specific information.

3 *A new friend*

This gives good listening and oral practice for students in a practical situation which they might meet in real life. Like all listening activities at this stage, students need a lot of exposure to the recording to enable them to develop their listening skills.

4 *Checklist*

This checklist is very important and you should go over all the statements of attainment in the classroom, so that students are clear about what skills they have developed. It is also another opportunity for further practice of the new language and structures.

Unidad 2 *¿Quién es quién?*

Functions

- Saying what your nationality is
- Saying what you do
- Meeting the family and introducing people

Grammar

- Gender
- Present tense: **tener**
- Possessive adjectives

Vocabulary

- Nationalities
- Professions
- Family members

Revision

- Countries/Cities: **¿Dónde está?** vive en, vivo, vives

Así se habla

1
Soy argentina

1

Input

As the first stage in the graded input, give the names of the countries and get the students to repeat them chorally and then individually. If you have pictures of flags of the respective countries, you could practise using the adjectives of nationality, through further graded questions.

Consolidation

Check the meaning of the adjectives of nationality and use the opportunity to focus on patterns of pronunciation. Highlight the fact that capital letters are not used for nationalities in Spanish.

2

Play the recording several times to give students a good opportunity to hear the new sounds, before getting them to repeat the dialogues.

Consolidation

Now that the meanings of the adjectives have been taught, it is time to introduce the notion of 'gender' linked to adjectival agreement.

Note: It is worthwhile taking a little time to reinforce the fact that in Spanish, as in most other European languages, objects are classified according to a notion of gender – some objects are deemed to be male and others female.

3

Input

Get students to do the activity and work out the different adjectives of nationality.

4

Production

Students prepare the questions they would need to ask and the answers they would get for each of the characters. They can then take it in turns to be each of the personalities and practise further in pairs. Worksheet 2.1 provides further practice for students.

5 *Y ahora tú*

You can now move on to asking students about their own nationality. Start with yourself: **Soy escocés. ¿Tú?** Then turn to a student and ask: **¿Y tú, de qué nacionalidad eres?** The student will almost certainly reply using the correct pattern: **Soy ... inglés.** You can now use this answer as a model for the rest of the class and go round asking what nationality they are.

6

Listening practice

This activity can serve as the basis for a more extended piece of writing in which students write down a few sentences about the names of the characters and their nationalities.

> *Así se dice*

Consolidation

The question forms in the third person need to be consolidated. Establish the rules explained in this section and then, to give further practice in use of the third person, use a 'round-robin' pattern: get the students to take turns, in a group of five or six, to ask the person on their right-hand side: **¿Cómo te llamas?** and **¿De qué nacionalidad eres?** They then report to the rest of the group: **Se llama... y es...**

7

Production
Students use the visual clues to identify the nationality of the characters in the pictures. This activity should be done orally first and then written.

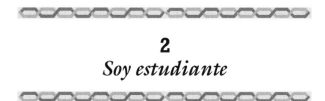

2
Soy estudiante

Input
Using OHT/Flashcards 2.2, introduce the different occupations by means of a graded presentation.

1

Practice
Students match up the jobs with the illustrations in the book.

2

In order to consolidate the new language and to develop the concept of gender for jobs, students complete the chart with the missing genders. The completed chart can then be used to illustrate the pattern.

3

Listening practice
Play the recording and get students to identify the correct job for each of the interviewees. Stress that it is not important for the students to understand every single word, but that they should be listening for familiar language/expressions. This kind of listening activity is extremely important for beginners, who are learning to identify key information.

4

Input
Note: In learning to ask the correct question, students need to hear the question being asked and to have opportunities to practise them themselves.

Play the recording several times, pausing between each interview to go back and review the language used. Now that students understand the occupations, concentrate on the questions asked and on the form of the verb used to give the answer: **Soy...**

Así se dice

Consolidation
Look at the questions in written form in the book and highlight the pattern and the alternative ways of asking the same question. Stress the difference between the **tú** form and **usted**.

Note: Always try to elicit a rule from the students first, so that they have to hypothesize about the pattern. In this way, they are forced to compare the correct model with their own model of the pattern in question, rather than trying to make sense of an abstract rule.

5 *Y ahora tú*

In groups, students can use the 'round-robin' pattern to ask the person sitting to their right: **¿A qué te dedicas?** and **¿Qué haces?** They can then present that person to the rest of the group, using: **Es...**

6

Practice
Further practice in using the third person form of the verb can be given by going back to Activity 3. You could also allocate the occupations to imaginary characters and build the information into two information-gap paircards. Students then fill in the gaps in their own card by asking their partner appropriate questions and by giving the appropriate answer when asked.

7

Practice
Further practice can be given by students questioning each other about their friends, as suggested. In pairs, they take turns to ask, for example: **¿Cómo se llama tu amigo/a? ¿A qué se dedica?** They should be encouraged to improvize. Additionally, samples of the information obtained can be reported back to the rest of the class.

Así se dice

Consolidation
This shows a range of typical questions which might be encountered by visitors to a Spanish-speaking country. It is worthwhile going through these and highlighting their meaning. Once more, it is better to encourage students to guess at the meaning and to confirm or reject their notions, rather than simply to 'tell' them.

8

Listening practice
Play the recording through several times, pausing to allow the students time to absorb the information. After

each interview, it may be appropriate for you to ask a series of graded questions to assist students in making sense of what they hear. For example, after the first interview you could ask: **¿Se llama Sandra Patricia o se llama Ana María?** and **¿Trabaja en una oficina o en una óptica?** before asking target questions.

9

Production
Students do the activity based on the illustrations. Again, you may find it necessary to go over the example with the class first, to ensure that they understand the task. In particular, you need to elicit from them the meaning of **pero**. It is worthwhile highlighting the pronunciation of **pero** and distinguishing it from **perro**, as the pronunciation of **r** and **rr** in Spanish is often a source of difficulty for speakers of English.

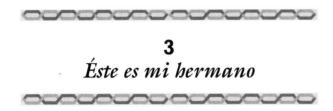

3
Éste es mi hermano

1

Input
Using the family tree on Worksheet 2.3, do a graded presentation of the members of the family using **se llama**: **El abuelo se llama José Martínez. ¿Sí o no?** Then ask alternative questions, followed by the target question: **¿Cómo se llama el padre de Miguel García?** In this way, the members of the family can be introduced, before moving on to the consolidation activity suggested in the book.

2

Practice
After exploring the Mafalda cartoon, students could try presenting the characters in Activity 8 of the previous section, using the same formula: **Éste/a es...**

> *Así se dice*

Consolidation
The form of presentation should be established by focusing on the formula provided in the book.

3 *Y ahora tú*

Practice
This activity can be extended to enable the students to point out other members of the family. The family tree on Worksheet 2.3 could be used here as the basis of

pairwork in which the students take turns at introducing a member of the family.

4

Listening practice
Play the recording. When the students feel comfortable with the new language, they can move on to the same kind of 'round-robin' activity as before, introducing the person sitting on their right to the person sitting on their left. They should be encouraged to greet the person they are introducing and to ask their name first.

> *Así se dice*

Consolidation
Present the way to introduce someone in a formal situation, using **usted**, together with the expressions of pleasure. Then students can repeat the previous activity using the full dialogue.

5

Listening practice
In order to reinforce the patterns for both formal and informal introductions, play the recording of a variety of introductions. Students could do Activity C in *Práctica* at this point.

6 *Y ahora tú*

For this activity, where students are required to present a member of their family, they might base their work on the family used in Activity 1.

7 *Los números*

Input
Learning numbers is a vital element of language learning since so much depends on them. Emphasize the fact that a great deal of practice is needed in order to learn the numbers, and that you will frequently return to numbers for revision. For this purpose, make yourself a set of numbered cards from 1 to 20, and then, by tens to 100.

The first stage is to play the recording and have the students repeat the numbers after the speaker. As each number is said, hold up the appropriate card, so that students don't simply use their aural memory, but also complement it with visual stimulus. When this has been done several times, chorally and then individually, use graded questions to rehearse the numbers thoroughly. Some other activities which help to practise/revise numbers, include bingo; counting by multiples; writing the numbers on the board and then removing them one by one, until none is left.

This box shows **tiene/tienes** and **tengo**. Students can use a grid like the example below to practise asking how many brothers and sisters certain people have.

	Jaime (12)	Alicia (19)	Jordi (15)	Montse (8)	Patxi (20)	Elena (13)
Hermanos	3	2	3	0	5	1
Hermanas	1	2	0	0	0	1

This can then be used as the basis for paired practice, in which students take it in turns to ask each other about the numbers of brothers and sisters each character has. If students take it in turns to be one of the characters, it also provides a basis for practising: **¿Cuántos años tienes?**

8

Listening practice

Give the students, or get them to draw, a simple grid into which they can insert details about Esperanza's family, i.e. the number and ages of her children. Like all listening activities, this should be done carefully and the recording played several times to enable students to grasp the specific information they require.

9 Y ahora tú

Production

Students can now get together in groups to exchange information about each other's family. Especially with adults, questions of age can be sensitive. You may judge it more prudent to assign each student a ready-made family about which to talk, by preparing in advance cue cards with this information.

▲▲▲▲▲▲ Temas ▲▲▲▲▲▲

Sueños a las cuatro de la tarde

Telenovelas

After reading through the passage, ask students the true/false questions below. Alternatively, you could write some multiple-choice comprehension questions for them as further exploration of the soap opera.

1 **La telenovela** means 'big industry' in Spanish.
2 Venezuelan soaps are called **culebrones**, which means 'long snakes'.
3 Corín Tellado starred in the first soap in Spain.
4 *Simplemente María* is the name of his first novel.
5 The story is basically that of Cinderella.
6 **Una campesina** means 'a peasant girl'.

7 María marries the son of the wealthy house where she works as a servant.
8 She is thrown out of the household for being pregnant.
9 María survives by becoming like her employers.
10 The heroines in every soap since then have been the same as María.
11 The Spanish for 'witch' is **bruja**.
12 *El derecho de nacer* was the first soap and was on Cuban radio until 1948.

Watching TV watching you

This section could be used for private reading by the students, where they work on a series of questions which they could ask about the statistical tables, using **¿Cuántos? ¿Dónde?** and **¿Quién?**

✦✦ Veamos de nuevo ✦✦
Gramática

1 Words for people and things

Consolidation

Read over with the students the section on gender in Spanish. Make constant reference to the examples they have already encountered when giving examples.

2 Words describing nationalities

The rules for adjectival agreement are examined here. Confirm or reject students' hypotheses on the matter.

3 I have, you have

Consolidation

The pattern for the verb **tener** is explored here and students can be made aware of its structure.

4 My, your, his

Possessive adjectives have been used on several occasions. The different elements are categorized here. Confirm or reject the rules which students have begun to formulate.

▪ Práctica ▬▬▬▬▬

A To be or to have

Further practice of the new structures is given here. Students fill in the gaps with the appropriate form of **tener** or **ser**.

B ¿De dónde son?

This activity gives more practice in using adjectives of nationality together with the previously encountered forms **es de** and **habla**.

C Let me introduce you

This activity gives valuable practice in introducing members of the family with **éste/a**.

D What was the question?

Students are required to produce the correct question for each of the answers given. This is a good opportunity to explore the full range of question forms which students have already come across.

E What's my line?

This quiz activity draws together the main points of the unit as students fill in gaps to reveal the name of an occupation.

▪ Un paso más

1 Applying for a job

Production

In order to make use of the language they have learned, students could do this activity, which requires them to fill in some of the details they might find on a job application form.

2

Listening practice

Using the grid given with this activity, play the recording and get the students to fill in the appropriate details under the headings given. Be sure to take advantage of the correction procedure, not merely to count correct answers, but to consolidate new language and to afford further opportunities for practice.

Unidad 3 *Mi ciudad y mi barrio*

Functions

- Saying what your home town is like
- Describing buildings and places
- Saying what there is in your town

Grammar

- Plurals
- Indefinite articles
- **hay**
- Adjectives

Vocabulary

- Buildings and places

Revision

- Countries/Cities: **¿Dónde está? vive en, vivo, vives**

Revise names of cities and locations, by beginning with asking, for example: **¿Dónde está Uruguay?** and eliciting: **Está en America Latina.** You can then progress to ask other questions such as: **¿Cómo se llama la capital de Chile? ¿Dónde está la ciudad de Caracas?** These questions can be graded, by offering alternative answers to students who are either unsure of the structure or do not know the information: **¿La capital de Chile es Caracas o Santiago?**

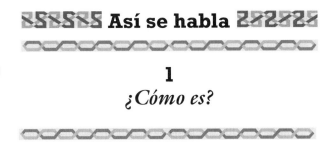

Así se habla

1
¿Cómo es?

1

Input

Play the recording of adjectives and encourage students to look at the pictures of **barrios** and **ciudades/ pueblos** and work out what each one means. Firstly, students listen and repeat. Given that all but two of them are cognates this should not be too difficult.

2

Practice

In order to support the students when they are doing this activity, give them a table like the one below. This provides them with well-known cities/towns, which they then have to match up with an appropriate set of adjectives, by asking a partner for her/his opinion: **¿Cómo es...?** If students are having difficulty understanding the target question, use alternatives or true/false statements to make it easier.

	pequeño	grande	moderno	antiguo	tranquilo	bonito
París						
Segovia						
Buenos Aires						
Edimburgo						

3

Listening practice

You will need to repeat the recording several times so that students can grasp the full text. Also, in correction, you will need to use different kinds of questions to enable all the students to answer.

> *Así se acostumbra*

Read this section with the students and highlight the uniqueness of the concept of a **barrio** and the associations it creates.

4

Listening practice

Play the recording for students to write down the appropriate adjectives used to describe each person's **barrio**.

Since there have now been examples of masculine and feminine nouns, this is a useful point to try to elicit from the students the fact that the ending on the adjective changes to match the noun it is describing.

Note: Match the language you use to explain this concept to the level of understanding of your students.

5 *Y ahora tú*

You can now move on to asking students to describe their own **barrio**. One way to do this is to start with yourself: **Vivo en el barrio de Lee, en Lewisham.** Finally, consolidate the language which they have encountered previously and use it to form the basis of the new language, i.e. describing the **barrios**.

Turn to a student and ask: **¿Y tú, dónde vives?** The student should reply using the pattern: **Vivo en el barrio de Bow, en Tower Hamlets.** You can now use this answer as a model for the rest of the class and go round asking which **barrio** they live in.

Students can work in pairs and do the information-gap activity on Worksheet 3.1. Cut up the cards and hand them out to the students who find out the missing details by asking their partner: **¿Cómo te llamas? ¿De dónde eres? ¿En qué barrio vives?**

By referring back to the grid in Activity 2, students can also ask: **¿Cómo es tu barrio?** This should last between five and ten minutes on average and provides a valuable linguistic support for the new language which is to be practised.

Consolidation

The above activity can serve as the basis for a more extended piece of writing in which the students write down a few sentences about where they live.

6

Input

Now that the meanings of the adjectives have been taught, it is time to introduce the notion of 'gender', linked to adjectival agreement. This can be done by presenting a number of **pueblos**, **barrios** and **ciudades**, together with appropriate descriptions, as is done in Activity 6.

Play the recording and get students to read and attempt to complete the activity. Make explicit the fact that, in the same way as some words are **el** words and others are **la** words, so too, words which describe them have to be the same. This is very important for future development, since any errors at this stage will increase as the students progress.

It is worthwhile taking a little time to reinforce the notion of gender and to emphasize the importance, when learning new words, of classifying them according to whether they are **el** or **la** words. Reference can be made here to *Gramática*, where the concepts are explained in a more structured manner.

7

Production

Students can now use the language they have just learned to produce descriptions of San Sebastián, México and Almagro, before moving on to give a more detailed description of the city or town where they are originally from, as suggested in Activity 8.

9

Reading

You will want to develop good reading habits in students from an early stage and this activity encourages

two important kinds of reading – for gist and for specific detail. Begin with the easier activity, i.e. skimming for gist. To do this you can give students a grid like the one in the next column which gives them contrasting adjectives. They choose those which apply to Madrid. This can be done in pairs, with students taking turns to ask each other alternative questions, such as: **¿Cómo es Madrid? Es una ciudad... ¿Es una ciudad grande o pequeña?**

pequeña	❑	grande	❑
antigua	❑	moderna	❑
tranquila	❑	alegre	❑
bonita	❑	aburrida	❑

Students can then move on to answering the comprehension questions on the passage.

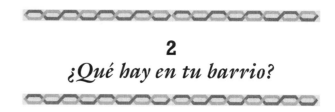

2
¿Qué hay en tu barrio?

Presentation

Draw an outline map of an imaginary town on the board. Introduce the following places in town in the order given below. (This can also be done on the OHP using a pre-prepared map with places being uncovered one by one.)

1 **el museo, el supermercado, el teatro, el estanco, el ayuntamiento, el bar, el parque, el restaurante, el hospital**

2 **la iglesia, la tienda, la galería, la escuela, la farmacia, la plaza mayor, la catedral, la oficina de Correos**

Introduce these places using graded presentation. Point to **el museo** (OHT/Flashcards 3.2) and say: **Es el museo.** The students repeat the statement, first chorally and then individually. Do this for all masculine nouns.

When all the places have been introduced using the first level of grading, introduce the second level, by pointing to the flashcard of **el ayuntamiento** and asking: **¿Es el ayuntamiento? ¿Sí o no?** Do this with all the places several times at a brisk pace, so that the students get a reasonable opportunity to practise pronouncing the new language.

Then move to the third level. Point to **el supermercado** and ask: **¿Es el museo o el supermercado?** Do this with all the places, several times, varying the place that is pointed to and the alternatives that are offered.

Point at **el bar**, asking: **¿Es el estanco?** Look again at the map and correct your error, by announcing: **No, es el bar.** Repeat this tactic for all the places, several times, both chorally at first and then individually. Finally, point to **el parque** and ask: **¿Qué sitio es?** Elicit the response: **Es el parque.**

1

Practice

As you go through each word, highlight the differences in pronunciation between nouns which are similar in appearance to English words, such as **parque/restaurante**. It is also important to stress that **el municipio** is the Latin American equivalent of **el ayuntamiento** and to encourage those students who might wish to use this as a perfectly acceptable alternative.

Así se acostumbra

Clarification of the concept behind other places in town, such as **el estanco** is needed, so that students understand the cultural significance as well as the meaning.

2

Listening comprehension

Students are asked to see how many places they can recognize in this recording. More able students can be asked to write down the names as they hear them. Explain the meaning of some items which have not previously appeared, such as **la Casa de Cultura, el juzgado, la residencia** and **la casa de ancianos.**

3

Input

Quickly revise the numbers one to ten before playing the recording once over and giving students an opportunity to hear the conversation before they read it. Then play it a second time with students reading the text. Stop periodically to give students an opportunity to keep up and to clarify meanings.

Hay is an extremely useful and important structure, which, because of major differences between it and its English equivalent, needs to be taught carefully. When the whole conversation has been heard for a second time, ask a wide range of general, graded questions in Spanish: **¿Hay una iglesia? ¿Sí o no? ¿Hay dos bares o hay siete bares? ¿Hay seis tiendas de comestibles?** Elicit the response: **No, hay dos tiendas de comestibles.** Finally, elicit from students the meaning of **hay**.

Así se dice

Consolidation

Read through this section with students and clarify the meaning and uses of **hay**. Emphasize that it is both singular and plural and the simplicity of its negative form.

This is a good opportunity to ask students for other question words which can be used with **hay**, such as: **¿Cuánto/a/os/as hay? ¿Dónde hay? ¿Qué hay?** and to elicit meanings and a few examples of use. This can usually be done in Spanish at this stage, by asking simple questions, such as: **¿Qué otra pregunta se puede hacer?**

Practice

Do the information-gap activity on Worksheet 3.3. Students take turns to find out what facilities each town/city has. The end result of the pairwork can be a written activity in which the students write up a description of each place.

Further consolidation and practice of **hay** can be gained by going on to Activity 3 in *Gramática*.

4

Practice

In correcting this activity, try to use Spanish most of the time and grade the questions when students do not appear to understand target questions. This can lead on to pair or group work in which students take it in turns to report on an aspect of San Telmo.

5 *Y ahora tú*

Production

Using the new language and structures which they have learned so far in this unit, students can produce a description of their own **barrio** or **ciudad**. If you anticipate that students are likely to have difficulty coming up with a range of facilities, they could use the symbols on OHT/Flashcards 3.2 as a prompt.

3
¿Hay un hotel por aquí?

1

Input

Note: The use of dialogues to input new language, particularly the kind which is formulaic associated with familiar situations, is very common. The treatment of dialogues follows the same graded steps as any other input of new language.

Play the recording several times, pausing to encourage students to repeat key phrases, such as: **Perdone, ¿hay un hotel por aquí? gracias/de nada**

When students are confident about the pronunciation, read the dialogue from the book and invite them to supply the missing items orally. By stages, remove items from the conversation, until only the bare bones of the dialogue remain. At each stage, students have to complete the dialogue orally with their partner. This might be done as below:

Stage 1: A: **Perdone. ¿Hay un hotel por aquí?**
        B: **Sí, hay uno en la calle San Nicolás y hay otro en la avenida J.F. Kennedy.**
        C: **Gracias.**
        D: **De nada.**
Stage 2: A: **Perdone. ¿Hay un hotel...?**
        B: **Sí, hay uno en la calle San Nicolás y hay...**
        C: **...**
        D: **De nada.**
Stage 3: A: **Perdone. ¿...?**
        B: **Sí, ... la calle San Nicolás y hay...**
        C: **Gracias.**
        D: **...**

3

Production

Students can now create dialogues in which they combine the new language with language learned earlier, saying what they want to buy and asking where the appropriate shop is (activity 2 can be used to revise names of shops). They should be encouraged to improvise.

4

Listening Practice

Play the recording several times to allow students to become accustomed to the language. Again, if this appears to be too difficult for your students, you could turn it into an exercise in matching street names to places, before moving on to answer the questions asked by the tourists.

▲▲▲▲▲ Temas ▲▲▲▲▲

La ciudad de los sueños

Get students to match each of the twelve statements below with the appropriate one of the four cities (Buenos Aires; Barcelona; Granada; México D.F.). In correcting it, you can explore issues which arise.

1 At the end of the 19th century it was the destination for many European immigrants.

2 Miró, Picasso and Dalí all began their artistic careers here.
3 Its original name was **Tenochtitlán**.
4 It is one of the most important ports in South America.
5 It is one of three elegant Moorish which date back to the 15th century.
6 At the heart of this city are the colonial buildings.
7 It is the largest and most polluted city in the world.
8 It has been a very important industrial centre since the 1870s.
9 It has a beautiful **alcázar**.
10 It was captured from the Moors in 1492.
11 The grass plains where cattle is reared are famous all over the world.
12 **Tango** music originated here.

Mi Buenos Aires querido

Listening

Students can listen to the recording and you can devise a matching activity in which they link simple definitions, in Spanish, with the appropriate word from the text. You should stress that the aim of the activity at this stage is not to understand every single word.

La Misión: San Francisco

Reading

A lot of the vocabulary in this poem will be familiar to the students - either because they have already come across it or because it is close to the English equivalent. As before, a matching exercise, this time linking up opposites, would be appropriate for the stage which the students will have reached.

Practice

This will provide a useful opportunity for students to practise pronunciation and, in particular, intonation. Invite them to work, in groups, on preparing readings of the poem. These could be recorded , if the facilities exist, and played back to the rest of the group.

Calle Melancolía

Apart from practice in listening to this song, students could be provided with a series of graded questions about the content, which focuses particularly on the use of adjectives - e.g. alternatives based on adjectives with opposite meanings.

Unidad 4 *¿Dónde está?*

Functions
- Saying where a place is
- Asking for things
- Talking about distances
- Asking for and giving directions

Grammar
- estar
- ir
- Some prepositions

Vocabulary
- Buildings
- Ordinal numbers

Así se habla

1
Está delante de la farmacia

1

Input

Present the new language: **¿Dónde está? aquí, enfrente/delante de, es éste/a**. Then, make a larger version of the map in Activity 1, which you can use as a model to attach to the board or to a wall.

Presentation

Play the recording while students look at the map. Stop after each phrase to point to the map and illustrate the position of the different places. Students repeat the phrases. When the whole dialogue has been heard, you can ask true/false questions by pointing to one place and asking: **¿Hay una lavandería enfrente de la tienda de ropa? ¿Sí o no?**

You can then go on to offering alternatives, before getting students to correct wrong assertions. Finally, ask target questions: **¿Dónde hay una lavandería?**

2

Consolidation

Get the students to look at the pictures and to confirm or reject their assumptions about the English equivalent of the Spanish prepositions.

Así se dice

Confirm the meaning of **¿dónde?** and the correct form of both the question and the answer.

3

Practice

Students work on the activity firstly alone and then use the information they gain as the basis for pairwork, in which one partner asks: **¿Dónde está...?** and the other gives the appropriate answer. This is a convenient point to look at Activity 1 in *Gramática* which highlights the verb **estar**.

4 *Y ahora tú*

First, the students work out how to ask where there is a post office, a church and a tobacconist's in Juan's neighbourhood. They can then compare their own efforts with the version they hear.

5

Listening practice

In order to give additional practice in using the prepositions, students listen to the conversations of people asking in a variety of ways, where the four places in town are. Be sure to ask as many questions as possible about the photo to give further practice within a meaningful context. For further practice of prepositions, students could do Activity 3 in *Gramática*.

Así se acostumbra

Specifying distance to a given place has its own pattern in Spanish and it is one which students need practice in, if they are to use it with any confidence. Read through the guidance given in the book. Then, in order to practise this, you could get them to do Worksheet 4.1 which provides a simple pairwork activity based on an information-gap grid. Students take it in turn to ask the appropriate question and to give the answer.

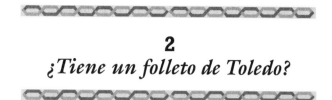

2
¿Tiene un folleto de Toledo?

1

Input
Using an enlarged version of the pictures in Activity 1, or an OHT copy, and a graded presentation, move from students being able to repeat the new language to being able to answer the target question. Input the various items which you might expect to find in a tourist office.

Practice
The above activity can serve as the basis for a more extended piece of writing in which the students write down a few sentences listing the things you can get in a tourist office.

Production
Students can then do the activity specified in the book, in which they rehearse asking for the items. This could be done as pairwork and then written down.

2

Listening practice
Students listen to the recording of the dialogues and try to identify what each person is asking for. Play the recording through several times, pausing to replay certain key parts and to highlight useful expressions.

Practice to production
Both the dialogues are rich in language which is fully accessible to the students. It is therefore worthwhile taking some time to work through them, by stages, in the manner suggested in the previous unit. This not only enables them to do the activity involving ticking the chart, but should allow them to go beyond it.

> *Así se dice*

Consolidation
Go over the new expressions for asking for things and highlight the pattern.

3 *Y ahora tú*

Students can construct a short role play in which they take turns at being the assistant in the tourist office and the customer and ask for the items from Activity 1.

4 *Los números*

Input
Briskly revise the numbers 1–20 by getting students to count around the class. Get them to count in multiples of two, then three, then four. Finally, get them to count around the class, missing every third number.

Using the same techniques as before, for the numbers 1–20, present the numbers 20–30. When students have grasped the pattern, move on to introduce 10–100, in multiples of ten. Once more, when students seem reasonably secure, get them to count in single numbers from 1–100. You should use the recording of the numbers as the initial input at each stage.

Use of the grid is important because it breaks the task down into manageable chunks, so that students are not overwhelmed by the amount of new language. Therefore you should encourage them to look for the regularities.

5

Listening practice
Lots of practice in listening to the numbers is vital. Begin with the **rifa**. Play the recording several times to enable students to spot all the numbers, stopping as necessary.

6

Practice
Read the dialogue with the students and encourage them to make use of the pictures to help them work out the meanings. This is the purpose of Activity 6a. Remember, all of this activity can take place in Spanish and there will be little need to go into English, provided you grade your language appropriately.

> *Así se dice*

Emphasize the use of the preposition **a** to indicate distance and direction.

7 *Y ahora tú*

Production
Using the model outlined in *Así se dice*, students work out the question they need.

Listening practice
They then listen to the recording and note down distances and other particulars of the directions. It is important to realize that this activity does not require the students to understand every word that is said. Instead, they are listening for particular information. Play the recording through once and ask a few questions, in Spanish, about the information given. Play the recording through a second time, stopping to highlight specific relevant information. Finally, play the entire recording through without pausing, to enable students to consolidate their listening skills.

Role play

Students practise asking how far each place is from Madrid. This can be done as a simple role play in which they take the role of tourist and tourist office assistant. They greet each other, and the 'tourist' asks about distance to the places specified in column one. Then they swap roles and this time the tourist asks about distances to the places in column two.

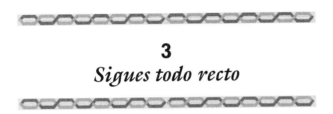

3
Sigues todo recto

Revise numbers by playing Bingo, for example. This need not be a complicated activity. Get the students to draw a grid of ten boxes in two rows of five. They then fill the boxes in with ten randomly chosen numbers from 1–100. You can then call out numbers at random and write them on the board. Do this until someone has completed their grid.

1

Presentation
After rehearsing the cardinal numbers, move on to presenting the ordinals. This is done by means of the grid in the book which students have to complete, thus demonstrating an understanding of the need for adjectival agreement with ordinal numbers. Further practice can be given by using similar activities to those used for teaching the cardinal numbers.

2

Input
Giving directions is an extremely important function in any language and time has to be taken to ensure that the students fully grasp the language. In particular, the pronunciation of **izquierda** can be problematic for English speakers. For this reason, clear presentation at the outset is vital. Use OHT/Flashcards 4.2 to introduce the directions: **a la derecha**; **a la izquierda**; **todo recto**; **al final de la calle**. Practise graded questions with these four directions.

Before doing Activity 2, give students an intermediate task to prepare them for the more complex directions. This can be done using Activity D from *Práctica*, the 'pacman' game.

3

Listening practice
Before playing the recording, ensure that students are familiar with the actual meaning of the questions. Then play it, taking the usual measures to break the activity down into manageable chunks – repeat sections and the whole activity in order to give thorough listening practice. Remember, at this stage, you are still teaching, not testing.

> *Así se dice*

Consolidation
Go through the summary of ways of asking where a place is and/or how to get there. In doing this, elicit from the students examples to illustrate the use of each structure/expression.

Similarly, work your way systematically through expressions for giving directions, paying particular attention to **giras/tuerces** and **tomas/coges**, which have not been highlighted, other than in the listening activity.

Concluding should also be dealt with as an important part of any discourse and can be built into the next activity.

4 *Y ahora tú*

Production
This should be done as a full role play and students should take it in turns to ask for and give directions to the places indicated. This activity needs to be prepared thoroughly and then performed for the rest of the class. Encourage the students to bring together all the elements of the topic and to elaborate using appropriate language from previous units.

▲▲▲▲▲▲ Temas ▲▲▲▲▲▲
Andalucía, ayer y hoy

This section can be treated as previous ones by means of multiple-choice comprehension questions. In particular, it is worthwhile exploring the similarities between the development of Castillian as standard Spanish and the development of standard English. Students may be surprised to learn of the extent to which Arabic culture played a major part in the development of Spanish culture.

Los romances fronterizos

This section can be used as a good illustration of how little Spanish has changed since the 15th century. Get the students to make a list of words which they recognize before preparing a reading of the poem. This can be done in groups of three with one student taking on the role of narrator, one the **moro viejo** and the other the **rey moro**.

La Andalucía gitana

Poetry is a particularly useful way of practising pronunciation and intonation in a foreign language. Lorca's poem is particularly useful in this respect since it perhaps lends itself more to expression and exaggeration than narrative prose. Get students to classify the language according to words which refer to emotion and the natural elements. Through simple graded questions you can explore the poem's meaning in greater depth, before asking students to prepare a reading for the rest of the group.

Los gitanos de hoy

Already, although students have only covered four units, you will find that many are not happy simply to parrot phrases which others have composed. The topic of gypsies today lends itself to beginning to explore more complex ideas in a way which students feel respects their experience of life.

Highlight the difference between **¿Por qué?** and **Porque** before asking: **¿Por qué se margina a la sociedad gitana?** Next, get students to provide the opposites to these statements:

1 Hay falta de comprensión. (No hay falta de comprensión.)
2 Son gente pobre.
3 Son gente diferente.
4 Sus costumbres no interesan.
5 No quieren integrarse.
6 Tienen una cultura diferente.
7 No tienen las mismas costumbres.

Students can then take it in turns to interview each other and to ask: **¿Cuál es tu opinión? ¿Qué crees?** Their responses could start: **En mi opinión... Creo que... Es porque... No es verdad...**

Finally, you can explore the issue: **¿Es España una sociedad racista?** in a similar way, completing this with a mini-debate in which each student gives his/her opinion.

✕✕◁◇ Veamos de nuevo ◁◇▷✕

Gramática

1 I am, you are + location

As with all grammar explanations, the most important aspect is that it should be clarifying concepts which have already been acquired, rather than giving abstract formulae. For this reason, the grammar section always begins by illustrating the functional use which students have already encountered, before moving on to examine the verb paradigm. In this way you can structure and add to what the students already know.

2 I am going, are you going?

This can be done in much the same way as Activity 1, by first getting the students to give examples of use from their own experience and then putting that into a meaningful structure, which illustrates the wider pattern.

3 Near and far

Working from examples which the students have already met, explain that these expressions all fit into a category of language called 'prepositions'. You can then look through them with the students, pointing out that they are remembered most easily if they are learned as pairs of opposites.

■ Práctica

C ¿Cómo se va a la catedral?

Students take it in turns to ask for the place mentioned and to answer using the directions given in the book. The activity should be fully elaborated into a role play into which students are encouraged to incorporate as much other relevant language as possible, including greetings and expressions to indicate the instructions have been understood.

D Play the game, eat the cherries!

Additional practice can be given here using a simple pair card with places in town (symbols or just the name) in one column, and one simple direction in the other. Up to ten different examples could be done.

■ Un paso más

1 Backpacker

This activity brings together all the new language from the unit. Students should do this as a written activity to begin with and then, on the basis of their answers, they can elaborate a role play.

2 Tour of Salamanca

Listening practice
Before playing the recording of the local directions for getting to the **Casa de las Conchas** in Salamanca, rehearse with students a range of possible questions which they might ask. Additionally, elicit from them the kind of expressions they might need to listen out for. Then play the recording in the usual manner, giving students plenty of opportunity to hear the appropriate expressions.

Note: You will begin to find that, through using this structured approach to listening and doing pre-listening skills, students develop a strategy for listening and recognize when it is appropriate to listen for particular detail and when a general sense of what is being said is all that is needed.

3 Latin American holiday

The passage describing Lima can be used in two different ways: reading for gist and/or reading for specific information. Which way you choose will depend on the time available and the level of your students.

Reading this passage for gist requires a lot of preparatory work involving the compilation of a whole series of graded questions about the content: true/false; alternatives; giving false information which students correct by reference to the passage; and target questions. When this has been done orally, set the students a series of target questions, to be answered in writing, following the order of the passage, so that, when put together, the students will have a summary of the passage.

Reading for specific information involves locating given items in the passage. Key words or expressions signpost the students and therefore preparatory work involves reminding students of the kind of language they need to look for – in this case distances and prepositions.

4 Checklist

Go over the checklist with students clarifying what is meant by each category and eliciting from them brief examples of what each area might include. It is essential to reassure them how much they actually know and to recognize that their active knowledge will always lag behind their passive knowledge.

Unidad 6 *Así se nos va el día*

Functions

- Saying how often you do things
- Talking about the time
- Describing your daily routine

Grammar

- Verbs: **-ar** and **-er**
- Present tense of regular verbs
- Reflexive verbs

Vocabulary

- Times of day
- Days of the week
- Meals
- Household chores

Revision

- Food and drink
- Use of the definite article
- Adjectival agreement

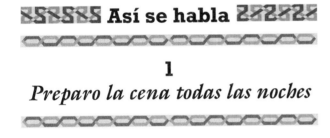

Así se habla

1
Preparo la cena todas las noches

1

Input

Introduce **el desayuno**, **la comida** and **la cena** by writing or depicting them on the board/OHP and using graded presentation to move from choral and individual repetition, through alternative questions, to the target question: **¿Qué es?** or **¿Qué tomo?**

Practice

Briefly revise food and drink vocabulary before asking: **¿Qué tomas de desayuno?** Students can then practise, in pairs, asking each other the same question and reporting back to the whole group.

Using OHT/Flashcards 6.1, do a graded presentation of household tasks.

Practice

Play the recording and get students to tick off which activity each character mentions.

2

Before embarking on this activity, it is important to do some preparatory work on the days of the week, as they are an important and recurring feature in any language. They are similar to numbers in the sense that they are regular and can, to a large extent, be learned through constant practice. One way of introducing the days of the week (and indeed months of the year and seasons) is as follows:

As early as is practical, introduce a routine at the beginning of every lesson of asking the day and date. Initially, you provide the answers, but gradually students will be able to supply the required information. Write the date and day of the week on the board: **Hoy es lunes 27 de marzo.** After a few lessons, you can ask: **¿Qué fecha es hoy?** and elicit the answer: **Hoy es el 30 de marzo.**

Then follow with: **¿Qué día es mañana?** and **¿Qué día fue ayer?** followed by **¿Y el día después/antes?** When all the days of the week have been established and written on the board/OHP, get students to read through them one-by-one, first chorally and then individually. Then proceed to removing them one-by-one until none is left. At each stage, the students recite all the days.

The same process can be used for the months and seasons.

Using the desk diary in Activity 2, get the students to fill in details of their own household activities. Their completed diary entries can then be used as the basis of pairwork in which they ask each other what they do on a specified day: **¿Qué haces los domingos?**

3

Input

Use OHT/Flashcards 6.2 to do a graded presentation of times of day: **mañana**, **mediodía**, **tarde**, **noche**.

Consolidation

Get students, working in pairs, to fill in the gaps in Activity 3. In correcting the activity, elicit and then emphasize the following features: use of the plural definite article to indicate regularity, e.g. **todos los sábados** (contrast this with the use of the singular definite article to indicate single action/event); adjectival agreement using **todos/as, una vez, dos veces, nunca/siempre**, etc.

4

Listening practice

Play the recording once so that students can begin to tune in to the sound of the voice. Then play it through a second time, stopping and replaying it after each gap, to give students ample opportunity to hear the expressions properly. Finally, correct the exercise. Use the correction as a further opportunity for listening practice.

Note: When you are asking questions, it is best to name the student whom you wish to answer, after you have asked the question, rather than before, as this forces all students to try to find the solution, rather than simply the student named in advance.

> ### *Así se dice*

Read over and highlight the features mentioned, getting the students to give examples of possible use.

5

Practice

This activity can be done orally to begin with and then in writing.

Note: It is important to circulate around the classroom and to check students' written work, as this frequently reveals errors/misunderstandings which might have gone unnoticed in the oral/aural work.

6 *Y ahora tú*

Practice

Design a simple chart with symbols of the household chores. Students then have a basis on which to ask questions and indicate the frequency with which they undertake these chores. In pairs, they ask each other, and tick the chart. Subsequently, the results can be written up in the form of a short piece of continuous prose.

7

Oral practice

Using **¿Cuántas veces...?** plus the appropriate form of the given expressions, students interview each other. They then report back orally to the group and follow this up by writing their own answers to the questions. This gives practice in formulating questions as well as in answering.

Listening practice

With the aid of the chart which they have just completed, students should listen to the recording and note the frequency and nature of the activities mentioned. In correcting this exercise it is useful to read over *Así se dice*.

8

Practice

As mentioned previously, it is important for students not simply to be able to answer questions, but also to ask them. This allows them both to engage fully in a conversation and to control the speed and intensity of responses. This activity gives further practice in this important skill.

9

Oral practice

Using the questionnaire, give students the opportunity to put it into practice, by interviewing at least one other person in the class. They will then have a basis for comparison, between the answers they have been given and their own answers. This allows them to say and then write three or four short sentences in Spanish comparing the answers. Encourage them to use **pero, y, también, tampoco, nunca, siempre**, etc. to build up more complex sentences.

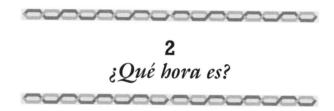

2
¿Qué hora es?

1

Input

Learning how to tell the time is a vital element in language learning. It needs a systematic approach and constant practice and reinforcement. It is worthwhile having either an old clock with numbers and hands which can be easily seen and manipulated by you, or a commercially-produced cardboard clockface. This is used a great deal when first introducing the time and at the beginning of subsequent lessons, to give sustained practice. Thereafter, you can ask the time during the lesson, at frequent intervals.

Begin by revising numbers from 1–60. Then play the recording and set the clock to the time indicated. Students should keep their books closed to begin with. Stop the recording after each utterance, repeat the question yourself and get the students to repeat the answer. When this has been done several times, move on to setting other times on the clock – all hours at this stage – and asking: **¿Qué hora es?**

Remember that if students are having difficulty with the target question, you can grade the questions and thus

avoid having to go into English: **¿Son las dos, sí o no?**
¿Son las dos o son las tres?

Repeat the times mentioned on the recording and put particular emphasis on one o'clock. When this has been done, elicit from the students the pattern that you use: **Son las...** for all times except: **Es la una.**

Así se dice

Consolidation
Read through this section and, using the clock, get students to give examples. Put the clock at 3 o'clock for example and say: **Es por la tarde. ¿Qué hora es?** Emphasize the use of the 24-hour clock for timetables.

2

Pairwork
Get the students to take turns asking each other the times, then correct with the whole group.

3

Listening practice
Get the students to fill in the times they hear on the recording in the central panel on page 64. This activity is more complex than the simple practice of listening to a single utterance, since the students are required to pick out the time from a number of other pieces of information. You need to play the recording several times.

Así se dice

Input
Using the clock, illustrate the times highlighted in this section. Go over it several times, to enable students to become familiar with **cuarto** and **media** and with **y** and **menos**. Practise using other hours.

Highlight the alternative but equally valid way of telling the time used in some parts of Latin America.

4

Pairwork
Get students to practise asking each other the times in the book. Then, use a sheet of blank clockfaces to give further extensive practice, where you read out times and students fill in the clockface appropriately. Give students the information-gap activity on Worksheet 6.3.

5 ¿A qué hora?

Input
When the time has been input and practised so that students are reasonably comfortable with asking and

telling it, move on to asking at what time a particular event occurs.

Play the recording and encourage students to use a combination of skills to pick up the information they need – reading the film adverts and listening to the recording. Repeat the section containing the target question: **¿A qué hora...?** and the reply several times.

Así se dice

Consolidation
Elicit the new structures from the students and confirm these by reference to the guidance given in the book.

6 Y ahora tú

Production
Either on their own or in pairs, students work out the questions and answers for the remaining events advertised. Once corrected, this can then provide the basis for a role play based on a telephone enquiry to the cinema, in which the students are encouraged to improvize and to incorporate other appropriate language into their conversations. These are then performed for the rest of the group, thus giving a clear functional outcome to the learning.

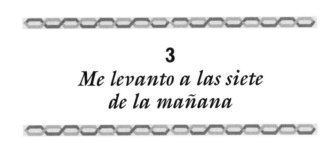

3
Me levanto a las siete de la mañana

1

Input/Revision
Before introducing daily routines involving the use of reflexive verbs, it is important to revise: **¿Qué hora es? ¿A qué hora...?**

Listening practice
Play the recording. Students focus on the illustrations in the right-hand column on page 65. Point to each in turn, getting students to repeat the questions after the recording. When this has been done a few times, make true/false statements and then alternative questions about the illustrations, in the third person.

Así se dice

Consolidation
Elicit from the students the pattern of question and answer and the form of the verb.

2 Y ahora tú

Pairwork

Students take it in turns to ask each other the three questions outlined.

> ### Así se dice

After a brief practice of asking and answering the above questions, each pair gets together with another pair. They then take it in turns to ask one member of the other pair for details about their partner's daily routine. This gives useful practice of the third person form of the verb.

3

Practice

To give further practice in the use of reflexive verbs, students can work in pairs, asking each other questions about the illustrations of Mari-Ángeles and Pedro. This can involve one student naming the activity and the other having to guess the identity of the character.

4

Students re-order the pictures into what they feel to be a more logical sequence. The process involved and the subsequent correction of the activity should provide an opportunity for lots of additional language practice using reflexive verbs, times and other common verbs.

Listening practice

Play the recording, stopping frequently to enable students to compare their version with the recorded one. Do not hesitate to add additional questions which might assist the students in their understanding of the recording.

5

To give further practice, students can be asked to transpose the account to the third person. Once more, this should be seen as a good opportunity to further practise the new language.

6 Y ahora tú

Using the model of María's day, students write an account of their own day. This should be prepared orally first, either through pairwork or by you giving a model based on questions put to the class as a whole.

7 El horario de trabajo

Input

This section aims to introduce important language which students will need to de-limit periods of time: **empiezo**, **termino**, **de...**, **hasta...**

Students may need a blank timetable to enable them to plot all the information they hear. Play the recording first, stopping after each character to allow the students time to absorb the information. If necessary, replay sections. Remind students that initially they are listening for specific information, so they do not have to understand every single word.

> ### Así se dice

Elicit from the students the patterns of the new language, before confirming or rejecting their hypotheses and then consolidating the model by reading through this section with them.

8 Y ahora tú

Students can now be set the task of asking each other questions to elicit information about their respective daily timetables. This is probably best done in pairs, with sample 'interviews' being demonstrated at the end of the activity.

▲▲▲▲▲▲ Temas ▲▲▲▲▲▲
El ritmo de vida

Un día de vida

Read over the passage with the students before asking them to match up the Spanish statements below with their English equivalent from the text. Finally, they can put the sentences together to form one coherent passage.

1 Hoy la influencia más importante viene de los Estados Unidos.
2 En algunos países las tiendas cierran a las 11 de la mañana y abren por la tarde.
3 En las ciudades grandes los horarios cambian.
4 En Méjico todavía hay siesta.
5 En América Latina hay otros factores.
6 El clima tiene mucha influencia en la vida de las personas.
7 El mundo hispano-parlante tiene su propio ritmo de vida.
8 La siesta es después de la comida.

Atardecer en la frontera

Read through the passage with the students and get them to write, in Spanish, Petra's daily routine. Some details may have to be imagined.

¿Dónde trabaja la mujer?

On the basis of the information provided in the illustration, students answer the questions set. Depending on the level of the students, this could be done in Spanish, using cognates and the question: **¿Qué porcentaje de trabajadores...** (e.g.) **son mujeres?**

A las cinco de la tarde

This poem, though apparently simple in content and form, provides an ideal opportunity to introduce an element of literary appreciation into your teaching. Explore Lorca's art by doing the following:

1 Read the poem to the class and get feedback on their impressions: Did they spot the repetition? What words struck them as being important? What seems to be the mood and tone of the poem?

2 Now, read it again, this time with students following the text in the book.

3 Consider some of the key vocabulary and its significance: What is the significance of **la blanca sábana**? Why is **el ataúd con ruedas** described as his bed? What could be the metaphor which Lorca is using? What could the **huesos y flautas** be referring to? **¡Qué terribles!** – what is being described?

4 Read it through once more and then get the students to prepare, in pairs or groups, an atmospheric reading of the poem, for the rest of the class. While they are doing this, circulate and point out elisions in pronunciation which students need to pay attention to, if the reading is to proceed smoothly.

Veamos de nuevo
Gramática

2 Reflexive verbs

Establish the pattern of reflexive verbs and then elicit/give some examples of use based on the list provided in the central panel on page 69.

Práctica

A Verb patterns

Practice can be given in manipulating the verb paradigms for regular verbs. Use this opportunity to reinforce the structure of verbs and to explore the grammatical terminology, as appropriate.

B A matter of organisation

Students do the gap-fill activity using the correct verb form. When they have completed the activity and you

have corrected it, the passage can serve as the basis for a further transposition from the first person to the third person.

C What do you do?

This provides an opportunity to use the range of verb forms in a meaningful context. Be sure to point out the structure of the plural forms of the verb.

D Question time

Get the students to do this exercise of matching questions with appropriate answers. After correcting the exercise, further practice can be given by getting the students to transpose the activity from first to third person.

Un paso más

1 ¿Está contento con su vida?

For further practice in using the new structures, get the students to prepare answers to this exercise on their own. When they have done this and you have sampled answers to each of the questions, use the exercise for groupwork, using the 'round-robin' structure.

2 Un día en la vida de...

Play the recording and get the students to chart it, by making notes of what is done against a time of day. When the information has been gathered via the normal listening techniques, students use the information acquired to write a piece of continuous prose describing the worker's day.

3 "Soy un amo de casa"

Students read the passage and answer the questions. This activity demands the skill of reading for particular information, rather than for gist. Encourage the students to predict the language which they might expect to encounter and, where necessary to make use of the vocabulary given in the middle panel.

4 Checklist

Read through the checklist and get the students to give examples of each of the functions mentioned. This needs to be done with a tone of reassurance rather than of testing.

Unidad 7 *Ésta es su casa*

Functions

- Saying where you live
- Describing your house
- Offering someone a drink
- Likes and dislikes

Vocabulary

- Addresses in Spanish
- Types of houses and facilities
- Rooms and furniture

Grammar

- éste/ésta es...
- gustar
- querer + infinitive
- Uses of ser and estar
- Regular verbs in -ir, -er and -ar

Revision

- Gender; agreement; question/answer structure
- tiene/hay
- ser/estar
- Shopping

Así se habla

1

¿Vives en una casa o en un piso?

1

Input

Use OHT/Flashcards 7.1 to do a graded presentation of the types of dwelling place: **casa**, **chalet**, **piso**, **apartamento**, **buhardilla**. Use the stages of question and answer which you feel are appropriate to the learners. If your students quickly grasp new language, you might wish to move from repetition to alternatives and then straight to target questions: **¿Dónde vives?**

Then get the students to match the pictures with the captions. This is a good opportunity to return to the question of gender and to refresh students' memory about its importance in Spanish and of the links which exist between indefinite article, definite article, adjectives, etc.

2

Listening practice

Students should draw two short columns, with five numbered rows, on a piece of paper. One column has the heading **casa** and the other **piso**. Play the recording and ask students to put a tick in the appropriate column to indicate the type of dwelling mentioned. In correcting this activity, use the third person: **El número uno ¿vive en una casa o en un piso?** Enquire as to the meaning of **pequeña** and **campesina**: **¿Qué significa, en inglés, pequeña? ¿Y, en masculino?**

Así se dice

Consolidation

Review the structure of the question and answer and take the opportunity to highlight the structure of regular verbs in the -ir, -er, and -ar groups.

Así se acostumbra

Read over with the students the explanation of the concept behind each dwelling name. Perhaps students have their own experience of dwellings in the Spanish-speaking world and it could be useful to encourage them to exchange experiences with the rest of the class.

It is important to consult the vocabulary in the central panel on page 73 in order to clarify the meaning of common abbreviations used in Spanish addresses.

4

Listening practice

Give students a copy of the blank form below for them to fill in the five sets of details. Play the recording. Students fill in the form giving the correct information. Depending on the level of the students, this can be done either with or without the visual support in the book.

Nombre
Calle
Número
Piso
Código postal
Ciudad

5

Input/Listening practice

Present the new language: **un garaje, un balcón, un ascensor, el aire acondicionado, el número de habitaciones, la clase de vivienda, la calefacción, la zona, amueblado.**

Students follow the instructions given in the course book and match the English phrases with their Spanish equivalent in the form.

When this has been done, play the recording through and get students to fill in the form according to the details. It is necessary to play the recording through several times, stopping to focus on the new language items which have been introduced.

6 Y ahora tú

Pairwork

Get the students to use the estate agents form as the basis for a role play in which they take it in turns to be estate agent and customer. They enquire about the type of facilities which are required.

When students have completed the preparation of the activity, invite some pairs to perform their role play for the rest of the group.

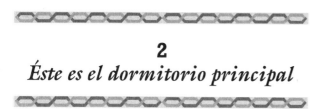

2
Éste es el dormitorio principal

1

Input

Using a graded presentation and OHT/Flashcards 7.2, introduce the new vocabulary of rooms. You may only require three stages: repetition, alternatives and target questions. Alternatively, you could have a bird's-eye view map of a flat with each room clearly identified on either side of a central corridor. In this way the new vocabulary can be introduced together with revision of known language:

Stage 1: **La primera habitación a la derecha es el salón.** (students repeat)
Stage 2: **La segunda habitación a la derecha es el salón – ¿sí o no?**
Stage 3: **¿La primera habitación a la izquierda es el dormitorio o la cocina?**
Stage 4: Make false statements for students to correct.
Stage 5: **¿Qué habitación es la primera a la derecha?**

Consolidation

Play the recording. Get students to number the rooms on the illustration. Follow the usual procedures, when playing the recording, of constantly stopping and reviewing key sections several times.

Note: You should also use the technique of highlighting, in advance of the listening activity, some key phrases which might present difficulties for the students. These are generally to be found in the central panel under vocabulary. In this way, students can listen with more understanding and concentrate on the new language.

Así se acostumbra

Read through this section with students emphasizing the enormous variation in ways of referring to rooms in the house, which exists in the Spanish-speaking world. It is worthwhile stressing that this phenomenon exists in all languages and eliciting from the students some of the differences between varieties of English in the US, Australia and Britain.

2

Listening practice

This activity requires students to listen for particular details, i.e. scanning. It is therefore important to do some preparation, before listening again to the recording, to enhance the students' ability to predict how particular information might be expressed.

In practice, this means revising adjectives to describe places, giving unknown vocabulary where it is unlikely to be deduced by the students and highlighting specific verbal structures.

Así se dice

Read over this section, not simply using the examples given in the book, but also eliciting further examples from the students. **Éste/a es** can also be used for presenting other people in company. Review the use of **tiene** and **hay**.

3 Y ahora tú

Production

Students prepare plans of their home to present to the rest of the group. If students feel uneasy about describing their house so publicly, it might be more useful for them to prepare a description of **la casa de mis sueños.**

4

Before playing the recording, revise the kind of vocabulary which students might expect to hear in the description of a house or flat. This can be added to by reviewing the vocabulary given in the central panel.

5

Input

Using OHT/Flashcards 7.3 present the items of furniture using a graded presentation. This is a good opportunity to combine the introduction of items of furniture with known vocabulary, such as prepositions: **El sofá está al lado de la mesita.**

6 Y ahora tú

Production

Using the new language, get the students to compose a detailed account of their house, or of a dream house. This can be done initially, or entirely, in pairs. It can also build on the earlier Activity 3, which concentrated solely on the rooms of the house.

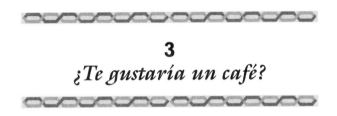

3
¿Te gustaría un café?

1

Input

Revise the food and drinks from Unit 5 – shopping.

Read the names of the drinks one-by-one, inviting students to repeat them chorally and then individually. This should be done fairly briskly. Now ask the students to match new vocabulary with the appropriate illustration in the book.

2

Listening practice

Play the recording once. Elicit the meaning of **quieres** and **quiero** and review the verb paradigm in *Gramática*.

Now play the recording through a second time, focusing this time on Activities a and b. Finally, elicit from the students possible meanings of: **¿Te gustaría...?**

Así se dice

Emphasize that in Spanish, as in English, there are many ways of offering food and drinks to someone. Read through the explanations given in the book.

Although it is important for students to understand the different ways of asking, for the time being they need to concentrate on one way of asking, which has a similar structure to other useful expressions for communicating likes and dislikes.

Practice/Pairwork

Students use Worksheet 7.4 to take it in turns to ask each other what drink they would like. The partner replies following the illustration in the second column of the paircard. The person who has asked the question then fills in the information in the first column of his/her paircard.

3 Y ahora tú

Production

When the pairwork activity has been completed and students have been called upon to act out some of the exchanges, they can move on to further consolidation of the structure by devising the appropriate questions for the scenarios depicted.

Practice

Invite the students to work out which drink would be most suitable in the realistic scenarios posed here, bearing in mind weather, etc.

4 ¿Te gusta o no te gusta?

Listening practice

Play the recording and get students to fill in the chart below showing the speakers' reaction to each drink.

(✓) = le gusta (✗) = no le gusta					
	las infusiones	el té	el café fuerte	el café flojo	otra bebida
Juan					
Rosa					

Así se dice

In going through the phrases, take care to highlight **también** and **tampoco**. Read through the examples given, eliciting further instances of use from the students.

5

Pairwork

For this activity, students make a list of the drinks and draw a tick chart two columns wide beside it. Then, in pairs, they take turns at asking each other about their likes and dislikes in relation to the drinks and ticking the chart accordingly.

6 Y ahora tú

Listening practice

Play the recording and get the students firstly to make a list of the drinks mentioned. On the second playing of the recording, students identify the speaker's attitude to the drinks mentioned and note beside each drink mentioned their own taste. In correcting the exercise, ensure that students have the opportunity to use both the first and third person pronoun.

 **Temas**

Vivir y sobrevivir

Más allá de las luces

Read through the passage with the students. Then get them to link up each Spanish term below with the appropriate definition in English.

ambulantes	inner-city slums in Argentina
villas miseria	makeshift shelters
conventillos	marginal districts
trabajadores industriales	young towns
barriadas	mushrooms
chabolas	Argentinian slum districts
criados	Peruvian slums
pueblos jóvenes	industrial workers
ranchos	street sellers
callampas	servants

"La casa nueva"

In addition to the suggestions in the book which follow the activity, a whole series of activities is possible in relation to a text such as this, including:

- Simple statements which the students have to identify as being true or false.

- Matching up vocabulary in English and Spanish.

- Matching up definitions of words/phrases with their equivalents in the text.

- Correcting false information.

- Putting together two halves of a statement.

- Being given the text which has been re-arranged and having to put sentences/phrases in the correct order.

- Listing all the words in a particular category – either semantic (all the words which have to do with celebrations) or grammatical (all the examples of verbs in the first person).

These activities do not have to be done entirely in Spanish and you may decide, in the light of the stage of your students that it is more useful, on occasions, to work from Spanish to English or vice-versa.

The important thing to bear in mind is that language-based activities help to develop deeper comprehension of the text and thus lead to a more thorough appreciation of the range of meanings embedded in the piece of literature.

Ésta es su casa

It is worthwhile exploring with students the variety and range of ways of showing hospitality towards others and highlighting as much the similarities as the differences. The development of cultural awareness is not developed simply by examining the ways in which customs and lifestyles differ, but also by understanding the level of similarity which can exist at the same time.

La historia del café

Students will be interested to read about the history of coffee and the range and variety of ways in which it is drunk throughout the Spanish-speaking world. If this is a theme in which there is particular interest, you might decide to explore it further through the medium of Spanish by using some of the activities based on texts which were suggested above.

Veamos de nuevo

Gramática

1 'I like it'

Review the structure of **gustar** and the examples given below the structural model in this section.

2 ¿Qué quieres tomar?

This explores the use of **querer** + infinitive.

3 Uses of ser and estar

Revise these uses with the class.

▪ Práctica

A ¿Qué te gusta?

Pairwork
Students take turns at asking the questions. When they have finished practising the singular form of the verbal structure, they can then move on to applying the plural forms. It is important to refer the students back to the structure of **gustar**, so that they can build the pattern in practice of how it operates.

B ¿Qué quiere hacer?

Get the students to complete the exercise practising the use of **querer** + infinitive.

C Mi piso

This gives good additional practice in use of the rooms in a house.

◾ Un paso más

1 Me encanta, me gusta y detesto

As an extension activity, once students are familiar with the basic structure of **gustar**, they should be encouraged to extend, by analogy, that knowledge to other similar structures.

3 La casa de Carme

Listening practice

This activity needs some pre-listening activity, before students are able to negotiate it with confidence. This can be done by revising some of the key vocabulary and structures which occur, before students listen to the recording for the first time.

4 Checklist

Go through the checklist with the students, eliciting from them examples of the various functions which are listed and illustrating the diversity of ways in which linguistic functions can be realized in Spanish.

Unidad 8 *En cuerpo y alma*

Functions
- Describing people
- Describing your symptoms
- Getting the remedy

Vocabulary
- Parts of the human body
- Health matters

Grammar
- **tener que** + infinitive
- **doler**

Revision
- **ser/estar**
- Reflexive verbs
- Articles

Así se habla

1
Es alto y simpático

1

Before getting the students to do the first activity, use OHT/Flashcards 8.1 to introduce: **rubio, moreno, gordo, delgado, guapo, feo, joven, viejo, mayor, alto, bajo**. These adjectives should be presented one pair at a time, in order to help the learners to categorize them clearly and thus remember them better.

Listening practice
Play the recording and get the students to identify the person who fits the description in the book. Expand this activity to get the students to list the qualities of the other people mentioned.

> ### Así se dice

Muy, **bastante** and **ni/ni** are important elements of vocabulary and it is worth taking a little time to clarify their use and to get the students to give other examples using all three.

2

Production
Students describe three or four personalities using the adjectives they have just learned.

Note: It is better to go for personalities, rather than private individuals, when encouraging students to describe people, for two main reasons:
1. they normally provide a common frame of reference and so the information can be checked to ensure that it is linguistically accurate;
2. it avoids individuals in the class being embarrassed if a fellow student becomes too familiar.

3

Introduce the colours using sheets of plain, coloured paper. This should be done using a brief, graded presentation technique and should last no more than five minutes. However, since colours are so important, you should be thorough in the beginning.

Present parts of the human body, focusing on the head and the physical features indicated in the central panel. Once you have done this, combine hair/eyes and colours.

4 *¿Quién es quién?*

Listening practice
Play the recording. Link up the descriptions Pedro gives with the characters depicted. Review the use of the article in describing the nature of particular features in *Así se dice*.

5 *Y ahora tú*

Pairwork
Working in small groups, students take it in turns to ask the person on their left: **¿Cómo eres?** and then to report the information thus obtained to the rest of the group. They can then move on to do Activity 5, describing their own physical characteristics for someone they have never met before. Students can gain extra practice by doing Activity 1 in *Un paso más*.

6 *¿Cómo son?*

Practice
Students return to the characters depicted in Activity 1 and give fuller descriptions of them, using the additional language they have learned.

7

Listening practice
Play the recording. Students will be able to guess the
meaning of four of the adjectives which are cognates.
The meaning of some of the others needs to be
checked, since they are 'false friends'.

8 *Y ahora tú*

Pairwork
This activity is best done by referring to famous people.
Students take it in turns to ask, for example: **¿Qué te
parece Gloria Estefan?** (You can make up paircards by
cutting out pictures of celebrities from magazines and
giving four or five to each pair of students.) Before
introducing this new structure, revise **¿Te gusta...?** so
that students can see that the pattern is the same.
Students can then move on to describing themselves.

2
Me duele la espalda

1 *El cuerpo*

Input
By means of graded presentation, introduce the parts of
the body, using an enlarged version of the dancer.

Practice
A whole series of practice activities can then be done to
reinforce the new items of vocabulary. These include
giving outlines of the body with blank labels attached to
the parts which refer to the new vocabulary. Students
fill in the labels. Or give out Flashcards 8.2, one to each
of the students, so that the others do not see which part
of the body is depicted. They then take it in turns to
guess the picture on the flashcards.

2 *¡Ay doctor!*

Input
Play the recording. For the time being, don't worry too
much if students do not grasp the structures: **¿En qué
le puedo ayudar? ¿Qué le sucede?** They should get the
general meaning. The meanings of the unfamiliar
expressions are in the central panel. Concentrate on:
Me duelen las piernas.

Listening practice
On the first listening, students should be encouraged to
find out which part of the body is being referred to.
Then they should listen for the particular expression,
which they might spot more easily if you tell them in
advance that it works in the same way as: **Me gusta...**

Elicit from students the expressions **me duele** and **me
duelen** and confirm this by reference to *Así se dice*.

3 *¿Qué les pasa?*

It is worth taking a little time to explore the indirect
pronouns with the students, by revising uses of **gustar**,
with which they are more familiar. Parallels can then be
drawn with **le pasa**, **le sucede**, etc.

Additional vocabulary is provided here to supplement
the other ways of describing symptoms. As in real life,
the ways of expressing pain are infinite. It is important
therefore to concentrate on the most useful expressions
for students and this often means the expressions which
can be used in many different circumstances, not just
when expressing discomfort. For this reason, **Tengo...**
and **Estoy...** are useful expressions to practise.

4

Practice
Get the students to do the information-gap activity on
Worksheet 8.3. When they have practised the activity,
correct it with the whole class and then get some
volunteers to perform the dialogue for the rest of the
class. Put emphasis on the need for appropriate
intonation.

5 *Visita al médico*

Listening practice
Play the recording, pausing frequently, and get the
students to fill in the appropriate information in the
medical record card.

6 *Y ahora tú*

Once students have described their flu symptoms, they
can take it in turns to be doctor and patient and fill in a
ficha médica like the example below. Encourage them
to use: **Me duele... Tengo... Estoy...**

FICHA MÉDICA
¿Paciente nuevo? Sí/No
Nombre
Edad
Estado civil
Número de hijos
Síntomas
Frecuencia

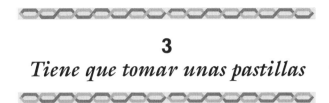

3
Tiene que tomar unas pastillas

1

Input
You could do a brief presentation of the new vocabulary here using examples of the real thing, or paste-ups made from magazine adverts. It is important that the students get some practice in using the vocabulary before being asked to do anything with it.

2 En la farmacia

Listening practice
This activity requires students to listen for information without necessarily understanding every element of the dialogues. This particular skill is best developed by discussing with the students, in advance, what the probable solutions might be. In this way, they will begin to develop good habits of prediction, which are the key to success in this type of activity, as well as being useful in real life situations.

3

Listening practice
Play the recording again and get students to fill in the gaps with the appropriate number of times medicine is to be taken.

> ### *Así se dice*

Review the structures for expressing obligation: **debo** + infinitive and **tengo que** + infinitive. Get the students to volunteer other examples which they might use, for example: **Tengo que estudiar**.

4

Reading/Production
This activity is aimed at testing whether the students have grasped the new vocabulary. It gives you a measure of the extent to which the new vocabulary and structures have been learned by the students and whether additional practice is necessary.

5 Y ahora tú

Review the expressions contained in the speech bubbles and the complaints, before asking students to do the exercise. In the case of those whose meaning is not obvious, ask: **¿Qué significa...** (e.g.) **hacer gárgaras?** You might even mime rather than simply provide the answer.

If students have dictionaries, they can be encouraged to look the word/expression up, though this should not be overused in the initial stages since it carries with it the danger that students assume there is a word-for-word equivalence between Spanish and English – a tell-tale sign that this is happening is when the student asks: 'How do you say "am" in Spanish?'

 **Temas**
La salud hace el hombre

La sanidad en España

Depending on the amount of time available, you could get the students to do a survey of their fellow students to produce their own list of priorities for healthcare. This can be as simple or as elaborate as time permits. It could also be a homework activity for students to write up the results for presentation to the rest of the group the following week.

La salud en Latinoamérica

If students seem interested in pursuing the themes introduced here, this can be done in a number of ways appropriate to their stage of learning. A series of simple true/false statements (in either English or Spanish) based on the passage, could be provided and students have to identify whether they accurately reflect what is written. A few key statistics could be written up in Spanish and the students have to find the English equivalent in the passage. Or, a list of Spanish terminology is set beside a jumbled list of English equivalents and the students have to match them up correctly.

La medicina desde abajo

A useful activity for developing confidence in the students' ability to make sense of Spanish is to get them to draw three columns on a piece of paper. Then, together with you, they read over the passage. When this has been done, they write down in the first column, all the words which they understand; in the second column they write down all the words which look similar in form or sound to English words; and in the third column, they write down all the remaining words. By this stage in the course, the majority of words normally falls into the first two categories. You can then spend a little time exploring some words from the middle section, which are usually words of Latin origin and building up connections, for example: **apariencia – aparecer – parecer – desaparecer**.

This helps develop good habits in learners, so that they begin to categorize new language in a more systematic way, which makes it easier to remember and gives them a strategy for dealing with unfamiliar words which they come across.

Se acerca la vejez

The poem by Mario Benedetti can be exploited for two purposes. Firstly, it provides a useful opportunity to practise pronunciation and intonation. Secondly, students can explore the language, using the kinds of activities based on texts which have been suggested in the previous unit.

✕✕◆ Veamos de nuevo ◆✕✕
Gramática

1 Ser/Estar

In order to consolidate the students' understanding of the differences between **ser** and **estar**, further categories of use need to be added. After reading through and commenting on the conceptual framework which is provided in this section, move on to activity A in *Práctica*.

2 You have to

This section reinforces the use of **deber** and **tener que**.

3 It hurts

Go over with the students the general structure of **doler**, drawing parallels with **gustar**, **apetecer**, **suceder**. Emphasize the way in which Spanish is not as 'possessive' as English about parts of the body.

▪ Práctica ═══════

A Ser or estar?

This activity gives students practice in manipulating the verbs **ser** and **estar** correctly.

B ¡Ay!

Firstly, students should fill in the parts of the body referred to in the five sentences. When this has been successfully done, they should practise the correct use of **deber** by matching up the symptoms and remedies.

C Another day!

Practice in the use of **tener que** is provided here separately from **deber**. This exercise also provides a valuable opportunity for students to revise use of

reflexive verbs. As with most useful practice exercises, corrections can be done in Spanish, with little need for recourse to English – except by way of brief explanation of potentially confusing points.

▪ Un paso más ═══════

1 Identikit

Working individually, or in pairs, students write out a description of the man in the illustration. Further practice can be gained from completing Worksheet 8.4 where students fill in descriptions of the various features.

2 El embarazo
Listening for specific information
Before listening to the recording, get the students to speculate about the likely expressions they should listen out for. Then play the recording through once, followed by a second hearing, during which you pause the dialogue after each element has been mentioned and replay.

Note: Although it can seem laborious for you, it is worthwhile playing the recording one more time when correcting the exercise, in order to enable students to hear the correct solutions, in context, rather than simply being told them.

It is worth underlining that **embarazo** and **embarazada** are 'false friends' and have an entirely different meaning in Spanish from the English cognate.

3 Centro de Salud
Production
This activity should be done by the students, initially in pairs. Rather than simply writing out instructions for each member of the party, they should be encouraged to prepare, in groups, a role play based on the situation, which incorporates as much of the new language as is appropriate. Moreover, given that this is a 'production' activity, students should be encouraged to improvize, by bringing in language learned earlier. The role play can be performed for the rest of the group.

4 Checklist

Go through the checklist of functions and elicit examples of use from the students. It is important to be encouraging at this stage and not to show frustration if students seem to have forgotten what you covered at the beginning of the unit. This only means that you need to try to recycle that language at a convenient point in the following unit.

Unidad 9 *Hoy es fiesta*

Functions

- Saying what you like doing
- Dates and celebrations
- Ordering drinks and snacks

Grammar

- **gustar** + infinitive (**encantar** + infinitive)
- Questions in the third person
- Use of **para**

Vocabulary

- Dates
- Drinks and snacks

Revision

- Food
- **gustar**
- Interrogatives

 **Así se habla**

1
¿Qué te gusta hacer?

1
Revision
Using illustrations of food for example, briefly revise **gustar**.

Input
Introduce the key vocabulary: **un parque, un parque de atracciones, una película de vídeo, una cama**. Then, using OHT/Flashcards 9.1 do a graded presentation of activities/pastimes. Finally, play the recording.

2
Listening practice
Play the recording from Activity 1 again, before getting the students to refer to the transcript in the book.

Así se dice

Consolidation
Read over the explanation of the use of **gustar** + infinitive (and **encantar** + infinitive).

3 *Y ahora tú*
Practice
Students can ask each other about their likes and dislikes using the model they have been given.

Así se dice

Pairwork
Read through with students the explanation of the structure needed to derive the third person. This can then be practised by the students working in pairs on the information-gap activity on Worksheet 9.2. In correcting the activity, introduce the plural form by asking, for example: **¿Qué les gusta hacer a Juan y a Ana?**

Students can get further practice of **gustar** in Activity 1 of *Gramática* and Activity A of *Práctica*.

4
Practice/Reading
Students match up the illustrations and the activities to give further practice in the use of: **A... le gusta...**

5
Listening practice
Students are listening for specific information during the first playing of the recording. When this has been done, play it again and get them to identify how often Juan does each thing mentioned. This is only possible for the first two activities mentioned.

6
Listening practice
This listening activity gives practice in scanning for particular information. As a pre-listening activity, get the students to list the qualities which Rosita's ideal partner might have. As students listen to the recording, they can fill in the age and tick the qualities which each of the young men has in common with Rosita.

	1	2	3
Cualidades			
Edad			
Activo			
Salir			
Ir de copas			
Cine/Teatro			
Deportes			
Parque			

The completed chart is not only useful for identifying the most appropriate partner, but it also provides an excellent basis for a graded question and answer session in which the students explore the qualities of each of the candidates.

7 *Y ahora tú*

Production

Using the structures and vocabulary which have been acquired so far in this unit, students can now put together a short account of their own likes and dislikes. This can be done orally first, and then followed up by a substantial piece of continuous writing.

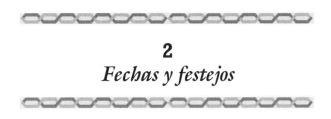

2
Fechas y festejos

1 *Los meses del año*

Input

Learning months of the year, is like learning numbers, days of the week and seasons, in that, to a certain extent, it needs to be done mechanically and repeated frequently.

Read the months of the year to the students and get them to repeat each one in turn. Now read them again, pausing after each month to write the name on the board/OHP. When all the months have been written down, explore the similarities and differences between the Spanish and English equivalents. Next, get the students to read them, chorally to begin with, and then individually.

After a few rounds of reading the months, remove, at random, one of the months and invite one of the students to recite all the months, including the one which you have removed. Subsequently, remove one month at a time and each time get a different student to recite all twelve months of the year. Do this until the board/OHP is completely clear, at which point, students should be able to recite the months of the year without too much trouble. This activity can be repeated

at the beginning of each lesson for a few weeks, until the students are familiar with the months.

2 *La fecha de hoy*

From the first lesson you will have been writing the date on the board/OHP, whenever writing needs to be done, so students will be familiar with hearing **la fecha de hoy** and **¿Qué fecha es hoy?** This activity sets the date in context and provides a range of other ways of talking about it. Get the students to circle in the book, or write down, the dates mentioned on the recording.

> ### *Así se dice*

Consolidation/Pairwork

Read over the explanation of how to ask for and tell the date and then do a quick practice session, using each of the ways. A simple, but valuable, pairwork information-gap activity can then be given to the students in which they ask each other for the missing dates on their respective paircards on Worksheet 9.3. It is important to insist that they ask for the date in a different way each time.

3

Listening practice

Review the important events which the postman mentions and which are listed in the book. Then play the recording and get the students to identify the dates mentioned for each of the events.

Note: When correcting the exercise, take advantage to give additional practice in using the structures/vocabulary in question. When students are not able to answer a target question, use simpler questions which they are able to cope with, such as a wrong answer which they correct; alternatives; true/false statements, etc.

4 *Y ahora tú*

Production

Students ask each other the questions which are listed. When they have done this, ask them to write up their answers in the form of a continuous piece of prose.

5

Production/Reading

Go through each of the festivals mentioned in the list and identify the correct dates by asking questions in Spanish. Get the students to write down the correct dates and then to read them out.

> ### *Así se acostumbra*

Read through the paragraph about **El día de los inocentes**. Students may wish to compare the festival with similar festivals in other parts of the world. This is important in helping avoid the temptation to see cultural activities from elsewhere as either eccentric or strange, and, by association, the language being regarded in the same way.

6

Practice/Reading

Get the students to read through the passages and then ask a series of questions, which are graded from easy to difficult. These can deal with the most obvious items to begin with, such as the date on which Christmas falls or what kind of music is sung. The questions move from simple true/false ones (**verdad/mentira**) to target questions: **¿Quién viene la Navidad?**

This kind of questioning can be very motivating, since it allows the students to follow the meaning of the passage in Spanish, without the need to use English. It also lends itself very well to changing the person of the verb which is used, so that, rather than simply asking questions in the second person to elicit an answer in the first person, you can also ask questions in the third person.

This should be done for all three passages and then students can be presented, in writing, with a selection of the questions which they have rehearsed orally. They then write out their answers.

7 *Y ahora tú*

Production

Students now write a short passage indicating how they celebrate the special days which are mentioned. If it is considered necessary, the answers can be rehearsed first by means of pairwork and then written out in full.

3
A beber y a picar

1

Input

The new items of food and drink need to be introduced using a graded presentation, so that students become familiar with the basic vocabulary which they are expected to manipulate. This can be done by means of OHT/Flashcards 9.4.

2

Listening practice

Play the recording. Students tick the menu board to indicate what has been chosen.

3

Input

Play the recording through a second time, concentrating on the expression used to find out the drinks that the customers want.

> ### *Así se dice*

Consolidation

Read through this section which highlights the key phrases for ordering drinks.

4 *Y ahora tú*

Production

This activity should be done in pairs.

5

Listening practice

This graded activity requires students to identify whether the orders listed in the book coincide with the orders which the characters place in the recording. Before listening, therefore, it is useful to speculate about what expressions students might expect to hear if what is written in the book is to coincide with what is on the recording.

In correcting the activity, do not simply accept **falso** as an answer. Instead, go to more difficult questions, by offering alternative answers, or by asking target questions, to establish the correct answer.

> ### *Así se dice*

Depending on the students' need to know, you might wish to explore in more detail the information given on asking about what food is available and what it is made of. In order to do this, you may wish to make up dialogues along the lines of those in Activity 3, and get the students to practise them.

Otherwise, you may consider that the students already have enough expressions to fulfil this task and be satisfied for this knowledge to be part of their passive vocabulary.

6 *Y ahora tú*

Production

Students complete the dialogue and work out the bill. Avoid the temptation simply to see this exercise as a mathematical problem. Rather, exploit the opportunity to refresh the numbers in Spanish. Get the students to prepare the dialogue in pairs and then to perform it as a role play for the rest of the class.

A further practice can be done as follows: Firstly, in threes, the students play the part of waiter and customers. They recite the dialogues as they stand. Next, part of the dialogue is removed and the students fill in the missing parts. Finally, only the first words in each alternate part is supplied and the students supply the missing elements. Encourage the students to incorporate examples of the use of **para**.

△△△△△△ Temas △△△△△△

El día de los muertos

Read over the description of the Day of the Dead. Then, go back and examine the pictures with the students, asking questions in Spanish about their content. As far as possible, use cognates such as **el cementerio**, **la tumba** and words which are familiar from earlier in the book.

The poem can provide good practice in pronunciation, particularly of words stressed on the final syllable, which can be a cause of great difficulty for English speakers. As in previous examples, students prepare the reading of the poem in groups and then give a recitation for the whole class. At this stage, it is not important to concentrate on the preterite, though this will be useful to return to later on in the course.

Carpe diem

Before reading the poem, it can be a worthwhile activity to provide a translation for each line, though not in the same order as the original. Now read the poem to the students, stopping after each line, and get them to match up the correct translation line with the original poem.

The second poem can be explored through a series of vocabulary exercises, such as matching up definitions and words; finding expressions which relate to time; and finding words which have to do with time or destruction.

La Semana Santa

The passage on the **Semana Santa** needs little comment, other than the testimony of a student who might have visited Seville and may have a particular experience to recount.

María Peña Alvarez

The diary entries for María provide a rich source of language for consolidating the structures covered in this unit. Prepare a series of graded questions on each entry and some of a more general nature. In particular, this is a good opportunity to revise the interrogatives: **¿Qué? ¿Quién? ¿Cuándo? ¿Cuánto(s)? ¿Dónde?**

✕✕✿✕✕ Veamos de nuevo ✕✿✕✕

Gramática

1 I like dancing

Read over the explanation of **gustar** + infinitive.

2 Who's it for?

Read through the explanation of the use of **para** before using the phrases as the basis for intensive practice of food and drink language.

■ *Práctica* ════════════════

A El ocio

Students match up activities with the illustrations. Once this activity has been completed and corrected, the new language could form the basis of a survey, in which students ask each other about their attitude to each of the activities and mark the replies down on a checklist, similar to the one used on Worksheet 9.2.

B Mixed up

Production
Once the dialogues have been rehearsed in this way, students can move on to more open-ended dialogues in which they supply their own answers to the questions. At this stage, they should be encouraged to improvize and to introduce elements of food and drink which have been covered earlier in the book.

C Odd one out

Students read through the different food and drink items listed and identify the odd one out in each case.

■ *Un paso más* ════════════════

1 La Noche Vieja

Students should do the activity suggested in this section and find out the required information about **el cotillón**. Much of the correction of this activity can be done in Spanish. A great deal of additional information can be gleaned from the poster and you should encourage students to do this.

2 Agencia Cupido

The listening activities require a good deal of preparation, including pre-listening tasks. Give students a list of unfamiliar vocabulary and ask them to match it up with known vocabulary or comprehensible explanations/definitions. Subsequently, give them a series of statements about each of the characters and ask them to identify whether they are true or false. Then ask them to make a list of the qualities/(dis)likes of each of the characters, before giving their opinion about the person in question.

When this has been done, they can then move on to describing each of the characters by firstly transposing the passages into the third person. They can then combine a statement of their own attitude to Eduardo Mendoza's character: **Me gusta... No me gusta...** with

a reason: **Porque tiene una buena posición económica.**

3 Checklist

Go through the checklist with the students, eliciting examples of each of the functions mentioned.

Unidad 10 *De viaje*

Functions

- Talking about travel
- Asking about routes and times
- Buying tickets

Grammar

- Radical-changing verbs
- Further uses of **para**
- Uses of **se puede(n)**

Vocabulary

- Time and travel
- Means of transport
- Types of tickets

Revision

- Numbers, distances, height, names, directions, etc.

Así se habla

1
Tomo el metro para ir al trabajo

1
Input

Before doing the matching exercise, it is worth doing a brief, graded presentation of the new language associated with means of transport by using OHT/Flashcards 10.1.

Get the students to match the names of each means of transport with the corresponding illustration. This activity provides useful practice and consolidation.

2
Presentation/Listening practice

Play the recording. At this stage concentrate on the means of transport and the reason for choosing it. If need be, students can be given a list of means of transport against which to check the one mentioned.

Así se acostumbra

Read through the passage explaining the types of train services on offer.

Así se dice

Read through the summary of ways of indicating how people travel normally and then get the students to practise, using the information-gap activity on Worksheet 10.2. In correcting this activity, take advantage to practise using a variety of interrogatives and types of question.

3 *Y ahora tú*

This information can be combined with times of day and other activities associated with daily routines, so that students put together a written account of their daily routine with times of day and means of transport used.

4
Listening practice

Before playing the recording, explore orally/aurally with the students the possible advantages and disadvantages of travelling by train. This does not require complex language if you use suitably graded questions to begin with: **¿El tren es rápido o lento? ¿Es cómodo o incómodo?**

The aim of the exercise is to find out specific information, so before playing the recording, draw students' attention to the particular elements of information which they require. This can be done by highlighting the structural signposts which need to be recognized, such as when the question is **¿Por qué?** the key information is usually prefaced by **porque**.

Así se dice

Language for enquiring about preferences is listed here. It is worthwhile taking advantage of the occasion to elicit from the students further examples of use of the structures in question. Further support is given in Activity 1 of *Gramática*.

5 *Y ahora tú*
Production

Encourage the students to write their own account of their preferences in means of transport and to justify them.

2
¿Cómo puedo ir al Cabo de Gata?

1

Play the recording, without using the book at this stage. Ask a series of questions based on the conversation to establish a clear understanding of what is said: **¿Adónde quiere ir Carmen?** (or, if this proves too difficult) **¿Carmen quiere ir a Madrid o al Cabo de Gata? Hay un autobús al día al Cabo de Gata. ¿Sí o no? ¿Qué hay en el centro de la ciudad? ¿Hay una estación de tren o hay un aeropuerto en el centro de la ciudad?**

Play the recording through again, this time encouraging the students to listen for the key information. They should understand most of the recording this time and this will help develop confidence in their own ability to understand 'normal' Spanish.

> ### Así se dice

Read over the explanation of asking how to get to a place. This can be reinforced by brief, simple oral/aural practice, lasting no more than a few minutes. With an outline map of the world, point to the place which represents your current position and say: **Estoy aquí.** You then ask the students: **¿Cómo puedo ir a...?** and elicit: **Hay...** (e.g.) **trenes.** Initially, the destinations can be relatively close, so that simpler forms of transport are probable. Then, you can move to further away destinations which might necessitate other, more advanced forms.

2 Go to Peru!

Production
Further practice in asking how to get to places can now be given. Students work together, in pairs, to prepare the questions needed to make enquiries about visiting places in Peru.

3

Listening practice
Get the students to draw a chart with three columns headed: **ruta, medio de transporte, duración.** They then list the destinations from Activity 2 down the left-hand side. Before listening to the recording, ask the students, in Spanish, to calculate the length of the journey to each destination and the likely means of transport: **Calcula la duración del viaje de Lima a Arequipa.**

4

Before doing the listening exercise, it is useful to give the students some practice in dealing with timetables and to input the main structures and vocabulary: **sale, llega, salida, llegada, dura.** This can be done using a simple timetable as shown below which focuses on the 24-hour clock. A quick revision of telling the time is necessary for this.

ESTACIÓN DE FERROCARRIL			
Horas	Salidas	Llegadas	Destino
07.30	Salamanca	08.00	Zamora
08.05	Zamora	08.15	Valladolid
09.10	La Coruña	12.30	Burgos
10.45	Vigo	15.20	Santander

The timetable serves as a context for introducing the new language via graded presentation, using statements about the movement of trains as shown. Begin with questions of the type: **El tren para Salamanca sale a las 07.30 horas.** Then ask: **El tren de Valladolid llega a las 09.30. ¿Sí o no?** Next, offer alternative questions, followed by the wrong information, which students have to correct, and finally target questions.

In total, this should take no more than ten minutes, but the time will be well spent as the students will then feel comfortable with the new language before doing Activity 4. Stop the recording where necessary, during the second hearing, to enable students to focus on discrete items of language. Students can then do Activities A and B in *Un paso más*.

> ### Así se dice

Review the ways of making travel enquiries. This can be reinforced by turning to *Gramática* for a fuller explanation of the use of **se puede.** Subsequently, Activity B in *Práctica* should be done.

5 *Y ahora tú*

Production
Rehearse this activity orally, before getting the students to write down the solutions.

3
Quería un billete de ida y vuelta

1 *Reservas*

Listening practice
Use the following chart as a support for this listening

activity. Then make up some additional **reservas** and read them out to the group. In correcting the activity, you can ask a wide range of questions and thus give further practice of: **Quiero hacer una reserva...**

	¿Adónde? (destino)	¿Qué día?	¿Qué fecha?
Nieves			
Juan			
Carmen			
Luz			

Así se dice

Consolidation
Highlight the difference between **se pueden** and **se puede**. Take advantage of correction to introduce more examples of **para**: **El tren para Salamanca**. This can be further consolidated by reference to *Gramática*.

2 Y ahora tú

Production
Get the students to work in pairs on this activity, building a role play around the diary entries and timetable. When they have completed the task, encourage them to perform the activity for the rest of the group.

3 Billetes de ida y vuelta

Listening practice
In this activity, students listen for particular information and select which of the alternatives matches the information on the recording. The aim is to encourage students to develop the skill of listening for particular information, rather than trying to understand every single word. Students can then do Activity C in *Práctica*.

Así se dice

Review the ways of asking for different types of tickets. These can then be practised by providing the students with small information-gap cards, showing a number of destinations and a symbol to indicate whether the ticket required is **de ida** or **de ida y vuelta**.

4 Y ahora tú

Students examine the bus timetable and find suitable travel arrangements. The information could be used for further practice in asking times and practising **sale/llega**. Students take it in turns to ask when a particular coach leaves/arrives: **¿A qué hora llega a Valladolid, el autobús que sale a las 9 de la mañana?**

Clarify with the students that, working on information gleaned from the bus timetable, they must purchase the appropriate ticket. Play through the recording for the first time, without pausing. On the second playing, pause after each intervention by the clerk to give the students time to fill in the details. Emphasize the fact that there is no single correct answer and that there may be a variety of ways of satisfying the requirements of the task. Play through the recording a third time and correct students' answers.

▲▲▲▲▲▲ Temas ▲▲▲▲▲▲

Trenes, buses y aviones

"El tren"

Read Machado's poem to the students. Then get them to put the words into three lists: the first containing words whose meaning they know; the second, those whose meaning they are unsure about; and the third, those they do not know. Go over the second list and confirm or reject their guesses.

Now read the poem again and this time invite the students to list all the words which have to do with time and travel, and all the verbs in the infinitive. By now students will have a clearer notion about what the poet is saying. Divide the poem up into three sections and get the students to translate a section into English. Finally, now that the meaning is clearer, get the students to prepare a reading of the poem.

Los buses

Time permitting, the section on buses in Latin America can provide a rich source for exploring different kinds of public transport. The chart from the bus routes in Lima could be used as the basis for revising colours and destinations/bus termini.

Los grandes viajes en tren

The history of the highest normal gauge railway in the world can be read in class as the basis of a discussion of travel in Latin America. Of additional interest, from a linguistic point of view, is the map of towns along its route. The map provides an opportunity to revise numbers, distances, height, names, directions, etc.

✖✖✖ Veamos de nuevo ✖✖✖

Gramática

1 Radical-changing verbs

Explore with the students the structure of the verb **preferir**. This leads on to the more general exploration of radical-changing verbs.

▪ Práctica

C Mystery destination!

Students can tackle the gap-fill activity to derive the name of a famous Spanish city: **Sevilla**. Do not insist that they work mechanically through each sentence before working out the name. Rather, encourage them to guess the name from as early as possible and to work back to filling in the gaps. In this way, the name of the city provides a meaningful framework for working out the remaining gaps.

D Coming and going...

Check understanding of these three important verbs: **venir**, **ir**, **coger**. Ensure that enough practice has been done in their use.

▪ Un paso más

1 Excursión con guía

Students use the new language in a productive manner avoiding simple translation. Get them to work in pairs and to put together a small dialogue containing the elements listed here.

2 El ferry

This task requires students to bring together a great deal of the new language introduced in this unit. As a testing mechanism, it can be done in English. As a mechanism for providing further practice, the questions can be approached in Spanish, by means of careful grading.

3A/B

In order to consolidate the new language, get the students to listen to the recording of train and plane announcements and to fill in the appropriate information. When this activity has been corrected, get them to go back to the earlier train timetables and make up announcements themselves for each of the departures and arrivals.

4 Checklist

Go over the key elements of the new language and ensure that students have grasped the structures. As with all checklists, there is a need to reassure students that they have the language to cope with what can appear to be complex functions.

Unidad 11 *Nos quedamos para el festival*

Functions

- Booking a hotel room
- Checking in and out
- Making complaints
- What's on and where to buy tickets

Grammar

- Past participles
- Radical-changing verbs (e – i)

Vocabulary

- Hotels and facilities/amenities

Revision

- **desayuno, comida, merienda, cena**
- Numbers, days of the week, dates

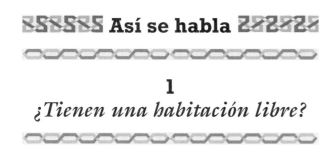

Así se habla

1
¿Tienen una habitación libre?

1

Input

Introduce the four types of room plus shower and bath using OHT/Flashcards 11.1 and a brief graded presentation.

Listening practice/Consolidation

Play the recording and get the students to identify the required information, as instructed in the book. This is a listening activity in which students are listening for specific information and, as such, it reinforces the new language which has just been presented. Begin with students listening without reading, and only after they have heard the complete dialogue, should they move on to reading the text in the book. This avoids the danger of students acquiring mistaken pronunciation of new words and thus developing a habit which is very difficult to eradicate.

Consolidation

Read through this section with the students and draw their attention to similar structures previously encountered in the course. Invite them to think about alternative ways of conveying the message. For example: **¿Cuál es el precio?** can be rendered equally well by: **¿Cuánto cuesta?** or **¿Qué precio tiene?**

Practice

Now use the dialogue as a medium for practising, not simply the new language, but the formulaic exchanges which are part of ordering/booking functions. This can be done as in previous units, by moving from students simply reading the parts to a totally free role play, in which they supply their own elements and incorporate appropriate language from other contexts. It can be broken down into as many stages as you feel necessary. The gradations of difficulty when using dialogues for language practice follow the same stages as the graded presentation:

Repetition: Students take a part and read through the dialogue, as it stands.
Practice: Remove key elements and phrases for students to supply the missing parts.
Production: Provide students with one word prompts and they supply the whole of the dialogue.
Testing: At this point, give students open-ended instructions for a role play.

2

Practice

Use the activity based on the brochure to give the students an opportunity to explore a realistic scenario. They can then go on to making further imaginary bookings based on a range of groups of different size and composition.

3 *¿Qué quieren?*

Listening practice

Play the recording. It may be useful, before doing the exercise, to get the students to draw up a grid based on the categories of facilities which they might require.

Read over the description of the range of types of accommodation available in the Spanish-speaking world. Students may have experiences of different types of accommodation and it is important to take time to explore these and to give the message that all contributions on this subject are both valued and valid.

4 ¿Qué servicios tiene?

Revision
Revise the language which the students have already met: **restaurante**, **bar**, **cafetería**, **tienda**, **televisión**, **discoteca**, **aparcamiento**.

Presentation
Use OHT/Flashcards 11.2 to give a graded presentation of the hotel facilities. While it may not be necessary to go through every stage of grading, some practice in repetition and in answering alternative questions is necessary before moving on to asking target questions.

5

Listening practice
Play the recording and get the students to note down the facilities. Before doing the exercise, get the students to list, in Spanish, the possible facilities which the hotel might be expected to have. This can be done by means of judicious questioning.

6 Y ahora tú

Production
This activity involves the students in bringing together all the new language which they have encountered in this section and putting it together in a role play. It is best prepared in pairs or small groups, with the students taking turns to be receptionist and customer.

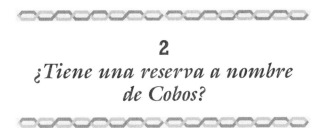

2
¿Tiene una reserva a nombre de Cobos?

1

Listening practice
This listening activity does not require the students to understand every single word, but rather to pick out the important information. Before playing the recording, explore, in Spanish, the nature of the information which Carmen might be asked for: **¿Normalmente qué información necesitan las recepcionistas en los hoteles? ¿Qué preguntan?** You can then elicit a whole series of question forms which students have covered previously in the course.

Then play the recording through once, stopping frequently to allow students time to absorb the information. Elicit the appropriate information and then play the recording through once more to help consolidate the new language.

Read through the guidance for using titles and forms of address in the Spanish-speaking world.

Consolidation
Go over the alternative language for booking hotel accommodation. Much of this can be used as the basis for eliciting the questions/answers associated with the expressions given.

2 Y ahora tú

Listening practice
Play the recording, stopping after each question to give the students time to work out their replies. Then play the recording through again, without pausing. Finally, correct the exercise.

3 Making complaints

Presentation
Revise the vocabulary for the facilities in a hotel. Using graded presentation, introduce the new vocabulary on OHT/Flashcards 11.3. Use the OHT to introduce the notion of **(no) funciona, (no) hay, está sucio...** Begin by placing symbols beneath the hotel signs and uncovering them one at a time as you make the appropriate statement about the facilities. Get the students to repeat the statement, then move on to making true/false statements, which the students have to identify, followed by alternative statements, from which the students choose the correct one. Next, make incorrect statements and get the students to correct them.

Practice
This can be followed by a pairwork activity in which the students ask each other about the various facilities in each of the hotels, before moving on to a writing activity in which they write out statements about each place. It is important that students join up the statements using **y, también, pero**, etc. and you should give an example on the board for them to follow.

4 Apartamento-hotel 'desastre'

Production
Get the students to look at the cartoons and identify the problems depicted. Do the activity orally with the whole class first, before they write out the answers

themselves. Use the correction process to give further practice in asking and answering the questions.

5 A la hora de salir

Listening practice

Before students refer to the text of the recording in the book, let them listen to the recording through once. Explore the language they might expect to hear, which will lead them to the correct information. Then, read through the beginning of each dialogue.

> *Así se dice*

Read through the structures for asking for and paying hotel bills. Link them back to expressions students have used already and elicit from them alternative ways of asking/saying the same things, using familiar language.

6 Y ahora tú

Production

The instructions for this activity should form the basis of collaborative role plays, by pairs or groups of students. As before, students should be encouraged to improvize and to incorporate as much language as possible from earlier in the course into their dialogues.

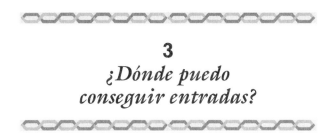

3
¿Dónde puedo conseguir entradas?

1 Eventos y espectáculos

Using OHT/Flashcards 11.4, revise/present the seven forms of entertainment. The presentation need not take long since most of the vocabulary items are cognates and can therefore be easily deduced. When you have done this, the students can move on to doing the activity as suggested.

2 ¿Qué hay para ver?

Listening practice

Play the recording. In correcting the activity, get the students to take turns at asking each other the appropriate questions.

3

Practice

Using the list of entertainments in Activity 1, get the students, in groups, to conduct a mini-survey about tastes in entertainment. The findings can then be fed back to the rest of the class.

4

Listening practice

Play the recording to give the students an opportunity to become familiar with the sound of the language before they confront the written text. Then play the recording again and get the students to identify whether the information given in English is correct.

This activity can be built on by moving on to more difficult questions based on the passage, such as giving alternatives, from which the students have to choose the correct one; giving false information, which the students have to correct; and asking target questions, such as who, when, what, where, how...

> *Así se dice*

Review the target questions which are likely to occur when enquiring about entertainment and venues.

5 En la taquilla

Listening practice

This activity offers considerable support to the students. Before listening, read through the text in the book with the students and get them to suggest possible answers. This makes the listening more meaningful and directed. Correct in the usual way and then get the students to do a quick dialogue practice.

6 Y ahora tú

Production

This activity requires the students to pool all the language they have covered in this section and to produce a list of appropriate questions for finding out about their chosen entertainment. Students should be encouraged to work with a partner and to produce a role play to perform for the rest of the class.

▲▲▲▲▲ Temas ▲▲▲▲▲
El gran teatro del mundo

El teatro español

Make the following true/false (**verdad/mentira**) statements to focus on the information about the

Siglo de Oro. In the course of correcting the answers, a number of issues can be raised and discussed with students, including the conquest of Latin America by the Spanish; the fate of the Incas; and the development of drama in English.

1 The **Siglo de Oro** was the fifteenth century.
2 The conquest of Mexico brought Spain great wealth.
3 The Inca Emperor was called Charles V.
4 **El Greco** came from Seville.
5 **Lope de Rueda** was the name of the first Spanish playwright.
6 **Lope de Rueda** was an actor.
7 The first plays were called **comedias**.
8 The figure of **Don Juan** was invented by a Spanish playwright.
9 **Lope de Vega** died in 1500.
10 His most famous play is **Fuenteovejuna**.
11 **Calderón de la Barca** was the most famous Spanish playwright.
12 **Calderón**'s most famous work is **La vida es sueño**, which means Life is a dream.

Man of La Mancha

Students can match the descriptions with the characters.

1 Miguel de Cervantes   a) el amigo de Don Quijote
2 Dulcinea   b) un caballero errante
3 Lope de Vega   c) el caballo de Don Quijote
4 Rocinante   d) una chica del pueblo
5 Don Quijote   e) el autor de la novela
6 Sancho Panza   f) un monstruo de la naturaleza

✖✖◆ Veamos de nuevo ◆✖✖
Gramática

1 Past participles

Refer to the explanation of the use of the past participle and the need for agreement with the noun. To reinforce the point, get the students to give more examples: **El banco está cerrado. El coche está alquilado...**

▪ Práctica

A ¿Servicio incluido?

Practice
In order to give further practice in using the language of booking/reserving, students should work, in pairs, on this activity.

B Guía del Ocio

If necessary, briefly revise the times, using a clock or a timetable, before doing the activity. Remember, this activity can form the basis of much more complex

language if you ask more difficult target questions, such as: **¿A qué hora empieza...? ¿A qué hora termina? ¿Cómo se llama el pintor malagueño...? ¿Cuándo hay un programa sobre...?**

C ¿Adónde ir?

This activity helps to consolidate the new language and recycle known language. Again, it is an activity which lends itself very well to further exploitation, depending on the stage of the learners. Ideally, you should ask, for example: **¿Por qué eliges la danza flamenca para la abuela? ¿Para quién eliges el teatro...?**

▪ Un paso más

1 La carta

Reading practice
Read over the letter with the students and ask a number of graded questions to check their understanding of the content.

a) Listening practice
Play the recording once over without pausing. Then go back and play it again, pausing after each item of requested information is mentioned, and examine the replies in detail.

b) Production
Students have to put together a letter combining the new language with appropriate other language, in response to the telephone message. Get the students to use the framework of the letter as a model for their own reply.

2 Quiero alquilar un coche

Reading practice
This activity requires students to extrapolate from language they have learned in one context, the structures and lexis which apply in a different one. In this case, moving from reserving a hotel room to hiring a car.

Firstly, students consolidate the language through an activity which requires recognition skills.

When the language has been rehearsed and the students can see that it is the same language being used in a different context, they can move on to more productive activities and arrange for the hire of a car.

3 Checklist

As in previous units, go through the checklist eliciting from the students appropriate examples of the functions listed. Emphasize the transferability of the language to other contexts and the need, given the lack of time available to adults learning foreign languages, to make the language they do know, go as far as possible.

Unidad 12 *Estuve en Acapulco*

Functions

- Saying where you went on holiday last year
- Saying what you did
- Saying when you did something

Grammar

- Preterite tense of regular verbs
- Preterite tense of **estar**, **hacer**, **ir**

Vocabulary

- Expressions of time
- Holidays/Tourism

Revision

- Geographical terms
- Pastimes
- Question words

Así se habla

1
¿Dónde sueles ir?

1 *Centros de veraneo*

Input

Introduce the new language with a graded presentation, using OHT/Flashcards 12.1.

2

Revision

Before listening to the recording, briefly revise **gustar**. This is a good opportunity to review Latin American geography and the compass points. Using an outline map of Latin America, get the students to tell you where different cities are: **¿Dónde está Buenaventura? Está en el norte.** Move on briefly to practise other questions: **¿Cómo se llaman las montañas que están en el oeste de América Latina? ¿Qué ciudad está en el sur de Uruguay?** The same can be done with a map of Spain.

Listening practice/Consolidation

Play the recording and get the students to list the activities which each of the characters likes doing. They can then write their own account of the favoured activities using **suele** + infinitive. Ask them, for example: **¿Dónde suele ir de vacaciones Hernán?** and elicit: **Suele ir a la ensenada de Málaga.** If students have difficulties initially with this question, offer them alternatives, using the same structure and give a sample answer, so that they can see the model. Practise this orally, before asking the students to put it in writing.

Así se acostumbra

Read over with the students the information about the holidaying habits of Spanish people. Again, this can be used to review compass directions and geographical features.

Así se dice

Consolidation

Read over with the students the explanation of the use of **soler** + infinitive.

3

Practice

Using the illustrations as the context for meaning, ask the students: **¿Dónde suele ir de vacaciones María?** followed by a question which requires the plural verb form. Highlight the changed ending for the plural. The illustrations can then be used as the basis for pairwork. Get the students to take it in turns to ask each other where each of the characters usually goes on holiday.

4 *Y ahora tú*

Practice

Further practice of the new structure can be combined with practice of the first person form. Get the students to do the information-gap activity on Worksheet 12.2. This requires them to find the missing information by asking their partner the appropriate question. It is helpful if you do an example yourself with one of the students so that the others can see the activity in action.

5 *¿Dónde fuiste?*

Input

Get the students to make a grid containing the names of the possible holiday destinations: **Cazorla, Cuba,**

Galicia, Brasil, Menorca. Then play the recording and get them to tick the grid to indicate where each person goes on holiday. The grid can then be used to ask questions to elicit the use of the preterite tense. Begin by asking: **El número uno, ¿dónde fue?** and stressing the preterite form as you give the answer: **Fue a Menorca.** You can then move on to asking alternative questions: **El número dos ¿fue a Menorca o fue a Cuba?** before asking: **El número cuatro ¿fue a Menorca?** thus eliciting the answer: **No, fue a Galicia.** Finally, you can ask: **¿Dónde fue el número tres?**

Take cards marked one to five and give them out at random to the students. Instruct them not to show them to anyone else. Tell them that they have to be the person who corresponds with that number in the interview they have just heard. Begin by asking one student: **¿Dónde fuiste el año pasado?** Elicit the answer: **Fui a...** Do this several times and then elicit from the students both the meaning and the structure of the preterite of **ir** in the singular.

Así se dice

Consolidation

Read through the guidelines for the preterite with the students. Make a special point of highlighting **estuve** and elicit from the students the possible origin of that form. For the time being, the students can learn **lo pas... bien** as a set phrase, until the preterite form of regular **-ar** verbs has been introduced.

6

Practice

Follow the instructions in the course book and go back to Activity 3, so that the students can get further practice of using the preterite tense. Again, for the time being, they will have to treat each person individually, rather than try to produce the first person plural form, which they have not yet encountered. This activity can be done as a role play in which the students take it in turns to play the part of the people mentioned or to ask the appropriate question.

7

Listening practice

Play the recording from Activity 5 again. This time, get the students to listen for the words which describe the holiday in question and to tick them off in the appropriate column of the grid.

8 *Y ahora tú*

Production

An example of a holiday, the means of transport, the participants and the verdict are provided as a prompt

for students. You could use this as the basis of a more sustained activity which gives extended opportunities for using the new language by making up cards with four elements: 1) number of participants; 2) destination; 3) means of transport; 4) verdict (show the level of satisfaction by smiley/sad faces).

2
Comí en El Panecillo

1

Input

Read over the letter with the students. Reassure them that they do not have to understand everything that is new. When this is done, give the students some graded activities to enable them to become more familiar with the key elements. It is worth beginning by focusing on the verbs in the preterite and asking a series of graded questions to elicit the correct structures: **¿Rosa Elena fue de vacaciones a Colombia o a Ecuador? ¿Lo pasó bien o lo pasó mal? ¿Estuvo en Quito o en Guayaquil? ¿Le gustó Quito, sí o no? ¿Qué visitó? ¿Fue a muchos bares? ¿Dónde comió? ¿Dónde más fue? ¿Adónde subió? ¿Dónde pasó la segunda semana? ¿Qué tal en las islas Galápagos?**

All of these questions can be made more or less difficult according to the level of the students. However, the general principles of grading apply. The easiest form of language is repetition, followed by true/false questions, followed by alternatives, then wrong statements which have to be corrected, before finally presenting the most difficult, the target questions: **¿Quién? ¿Qué? ¿Cuándo? ¿Cómo? ¿Dónde?**

Así se dice

When you have thoroughly exploited the passage, use graded questions to elicit from the students the regularities which they have spotted in the forms of the verb. Then read through the outline given in this section. When this has been done, you will need to move to a more systematic approach to the structure of regular verbs in the preterite. Further practice can be found in *Gramática*.

2 *Y ahora tú*

Use Worksheet 12.3 to give students practice in the use of the preterite tense. The first role play is the one described in the book, the others are along similar lines.

3

Input

In order for the students to become used to linking the preterite tense of the verb with the infinitive, give them a list of infinitives to tick off the activities in which Juan Carlos was involved:

¿Lo hizo?	No (x)	Sí (✓)
bañarse		
recorrer el parque		
comer		
subir a las montañas		
comprar		
ver		
dormir		
visitar		
pasarlo bien		

In correcting the exercise, use graded questions to keep the activity in Spanish and to give the students additional listening practice.

Listening practice

When the activity has been corrected, play the recording. Again, with the support of the chart above, get the students to identify the activities which have been left out.

Así se dice

Read over the translations of the new Spanish verbs which the students need for this activity. It is worth consolidating the structure of the preterite, by asking students to predict what other persons of the same verbs might look/sound like. Students could also look at Activity B in *Práctica*.

4

Practice

Get the students to transform the passage from first to third person reported speech. Firstly, get the students to underline all the verbs in the preterite tense. Then go through these with them, eliciting the infinitive of each verb in turn. Now, get the students to transform them from first to third person.

5

Listening practice

Play the recording. As with other listening activities, do not expect students to pick everything up on the first hearing. In correcting the activity, stop after each item and repeat, to give students further listening practice.

Así se dice

Review the first person plural form of the preterite. In doing this, it is worthwhile referring to *Gramática* to illustrate how this fits into the overall structure of the preterite tense of the verbs. Students can also look at Activity A in *Práctica*.

6 *Y ahora tú*

Production

This activity requires students to use the model letter as the basis of their own letter, written in the first person plural, describing a past holiday. This may prove difficult for some students, in which case you should give them the skeleton of a letter with gaps.

Additionally, you may deem it appropriate to give the students a list of the correct verbs, which are out of sequence. Their task then, is to put the verbs in the correct place in the skeleton letter.

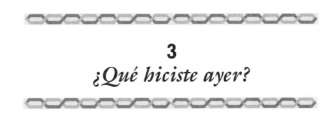

3
¿Qué hiciste ayer?

1

Listening practice

Play the recording through without interruption. Ask some general questions and encourage the students to volunteer information about what they might have picked up from the recording: **¿Qué dice Andrés?** Then read through the activities listed.

Play the recording a second time, pausing after each activity to give the students time to match what they hear with what is written in the book. Play the recording a final time, without pause, to allow the students to consolidate the new language.

In correcting the exercise, switch to the third person and elicit the answers from the students in the third person.

Así se dice

Input

Revise the times and days of the week. Then give the students the information-gap activity on Worksheet 12.4 and get them to work in pairs describing the order in which the different activities were done using the expressions: **primero, después/luego, y por último.**

2

Production

Using the illustration on page 131 as the basis for this activity, revise first of all the times. Then go through each stage to elicit a description of the illustrated activity in the preterite tense. You may need to assist the students, in which case you should ask a series of graded questions: **A las diez de la mañana, ¿se levantó o se acostó? A las nueve ¿hizo la compra?** to elicit from students: **No, hizo la compra a las once y media.** When these kinds of questions have been rehearsed, you can then go on to asking the more difficult target question: **¿Qué hizo a las diez y cuarto?**

When you have done this orally/aurally, ask the students to write it out in full while you circulate to monitor, assist and correct errors.

3 *Y ahora tú*

Production

Get the students to prepare an account of their activities on the previous day. It is important to stress for the benefit of the students that they do not have to tell the truth, but rather, that they should provide a plausible account of the kind of activity which they might have done.

They can then take turns in recounting, to the rest of the class, the activities of their partner, thus transposing the account from first to third person.

4

Input/Practice

Many of the expressions listed here have already been encountered by the students, though their attention has not been focused specifically on them. Get the students to match up the expressions with their English equivalents. It is worthwhile, time permitting, to revise the days of the week, months of the year and seasons.

5

Production

In order to give a meaningful explanation of Carlos's expenditure, students are required to describe his recent activities. This may prove difficult for some students, in which case you will have to prepare the activity orally first, using whatever level of grading seems appropriate.

6

Production

This activity is similar to the previous one and provides another useful opportunity for students to use the new language and structures with the expressions from Activity 4.

7

Listening practice

Students can practise using the plural forms of the preterite. Before playing the recording, elicit from the

students the appropriate expressions for each of the activities listed in English.

> ### *Así se dice*

Review the plural forms of the preterite with the students and, if necessary, refer back to the paradigms for regular verbs in *Gramática*.

8 *Y ahora tú*

Production

This open-ended activity can be extended further, by getting the students to prepare a slightly longer account of their last/best holiday, to include the places they visited, what they did, what they bought, where they ate and their overall verdict on the experience.

▲▲▲▲▲▲ Temas ▲▲▲▲▲▲

Hay muchas maneras de escaparse

La huida al mar

The information about holidays in the Spanish-speaking world could form the basis of a travelogue in which the students put together a series of recommended routes around the Hispanic world including six destinations. For students involved in a course where project work is a component part, this section could form the starting point. From here, students could prepare a resume in Spanish of their recommendations and use this as the basis for subsequent research into the destinations they choose.

También hay otras salidas

The theme of sporting heroes and ways out of poverty form the background for this section, which could also be the launching pad for a mini-project on Spanish-speaking stars. Students could put together a series of biopics on the stars mentioned. This gives good practice in use of the preterite tense.

"Deportes"

A whole variety of activities are possible based on the poem:

- Match key phrases from the poem with the English translation equivalents.
- Pick out all the uses of the preterite tense.
- Select key imagery and ask the students to explain it in English.
- List all the adjectives in the poem.
- Make true/false statements.
- Re-write one of the stanzas as prose.

Veamos de nuevo

Gramática

1 Talking about the past

It is worthwhile taking time to go through this section with the students, but also to remember that true mastery of the form will only come through extensive exposure and opportunities for practice. Read through the explanation of the use of the preterite tense. Establish the fact that the majority of verbs follow a regular pattern. Remind them that, in Spanish, we know who is speaking or being referred to by the ending of the verb. This is true in the present tense – get the students to give you some examples from the present tense of regular verbs. Emphasize that this is also the case when the future or the past is being referred to.

▪ *Práctica*

A Unas vacaciones estupendas

To give further practice in the use of the third and first person singular of the preterite tense, get the students to prepare, in pairs, an account of the holiday in Nerja. To do this, they need to transform the passage from first person to third person.

B Matchmaking

In order to give further practice in the use of the preterite, get the students to match the two parts of each sentence.

Consolidation

Many students will still be struggling with the overall concept of the verbal paradigm. It is useful therefore, at this stage, to take time when correcting this activity to review the verb paradigms and highlight, on the board/OHP, the concept of singular and plural and first, second and third person of the verb. Do not put up the whole verb at once but elicit from the students all the singular forms, emphasizing the importance of the endings and then move on to the plural forms.

▪ *Un paso más*

1 Matalascañas

Further work on the use of the first person singular of the preterite tense can be done by more advanced students, based on this activity.

2 El diario de a bordo

Reading practice

This reading activity, though challenging, will stimulate the more advanced students and should assist in the development of dictionary skills. Do not ask the students to translate the entire passage, but rather to focus on the particular language they need to answer the questions on the diary contents.

3 Por México

Listening practice

The true/false listening activity can be tackled either as a whole-class activity, or as an individual, extension activity for more advanced students.

4 Checklist

Go through the checklist in the usual manner, eliciting from the students examples of the various functions listed here.

Unidad 13 *Cuando era joven*

Functions

- Saying what sports you liked when you were younger
- Saying what you used to do; what people were like
- Contrasting the present with the past

Grammar

- Imperfect tense of regular verbs
- Imperfect tense of **ser, ver, ir**

Vocabulary

- Sports/Pastimes

Revision

- Descriptions, likes, dislikes, daily routines

Así se habla

1
¿Practicas algún deporte?

1

Input

Use graded presentation and OHT/Flashcards 13.1 to introduce sports. Firstly introduce sports which go with **practico...** When you have been through the appropriate stages of grading, move on to introducing sports which go with **juego al/a la...** When this has been completed, mix the sports and ask: **¿Qué hago?**

2

Listening practice

Give the students a grid with symbols of the sports on it and get them to number each sport in the order on the recording and to add information about the frequency with which they are practised.

> ### Así se dice

Consolidation

Elicit from the students the fact that some sports use **practicar** and others use **jugar a**.

3

Reading practice

Read over the passage with the students. Stress the fact that they do not need to understand everything. Tell them the meaning of **ha sido**. At this point there are two possibilities: 1) Use the reading activity as a test and get the students to work alone on the passage, translating and slowly deciphering the meaning.
2) Use the reading activity as the basis for the following practice:

1 Get the students to take it in turns to read the passage aloud.
2 Select key words in the passage and get students to link them up with synonyms and definitions.
3 Using different levels of grading, ask a series of questions to elicit the meaning of key ideas.
4 Do a transformation exercise whereby the students work in pairs and change sections of the passage from third person into the first person.
5 Answer the questions in the book.

4 *Y ahora tú*

Production

The questions which students are required to answer here can be set out in the form of a grid. Working in small groups, students take it in turns to conduct a mini-survey by asking each other the appropriate questions, and then marking the responses in the grid with a tick or a cross.

They can then prepare a report for the rest of the group. Depending on the learner, the report can take the form of simple statements or more complex statistics: **Seis personas practican el golf. – El 50% del grupo juega al golf.**

5

Input

Play through the recording and then go back and play only the first part where Isabel talks about the present. Ask: **¿Qué deporte le gusta? ¿Qué deporte practica?** Then ask members of the class the same questions about themselves.

Now play the second part of the recording with the students following it in their book. Clarify the meaning of **más joven**. Using graded questions ask: **Cuando Isabel era más joven, le gustaban los deportes. ¿Sí o no? ¿Le gustaba a Isabel el judo o el karate? ¿Le gustaba el fútbol? ¿Qué deporte le gustaba cuando era joven?**

As with all graded questions, if the students are having difficulty, move to an easier level of questioning, or, if the questions are too easy, to a more difficult level.

Así se dice

Consolidation
When the questions have been covered, elicit from the students the meanings of **era(s)**, **gustaba(n)**, **tenía**, **encantaba**. You can then go to page 145 and read through with the students the structure of the imperfect in Spanish and its uses.

6 Υ ahora tú

Practice
In order to practise the imperfect tense, get the students to interview each other, using the questions in the book, and to tick the chart below accordingly.

Cuando eras joven... (✓) = sí (x) = no	Juan	Mari	Ion
a) ¿Ibas a la piscina?			
b) ¿Ibas a la escuela?			
c) ¿Hacías los deberes?			
d) ¿Jugabas con los vecinos?			
e) ¿Jugabas al fútbol o al tenis?			
f) ¿Qué otras cosas te gustaba hacer?			

They can then move on to reporting to a larger group about the habits/likes of the person they interviewed.

2
Los sábados salía con mis amigos

1

Listening practice
Before playing the recording, read over the questions which the students are asked to answer. Give them a grid with the key vocabulary in the questions and elicit the English equivalents – this can be done by matching up the key English words and their Spanish equivalents.

Now play the recording over once. Check what students have understood against the questions they were asked. This can be done by means of oral questions or by giving a list of true/false written statements for the students to consider, in pairs.

Play the recording over a second time, stopping after the information relating to each of the initial questions

is mentioned. If necessary, replay the section of the recording before eliciting the correct answer.

Así se dice

Consolidation
Read over the examples of the imperfect tense with the students and elicit from them the infinitive of the verbs mentioned. It may be useful at this stage to review the structure of the verb in the present tense.

2

Reading practice
Read over the interview with Andy García and get the students to match up key words and definitions:

1 fueron	a) exclusivamente
2 exiliado	b) actividades preferidas en el tiempo libre
3 pequeño	c) lo que se ve en el cine
4 únicamente	d) lo contrario de grande
5 aficiones	e) tercera persona plural del pretérito de ir
6 película	f) una persona que no puede vivir en su país

Use the passage for further practice in the use of the imperfect and preterite tenses. Do an oral/aural question and answer session and get the students to answer the questions following the exercise.

Practice
Ask the students to work together in pairs making up an interview with another personality. They then perform the role play for the rest of the group who have to identify the person in question.

3 Υ ahora tú

Production
Students should prepare the answers to the questions together and try to make them as elaborate as possible. It is often useful to remind students that there is no 'lie detector test' for these activities and that the main purpose is to give them an opportunity to put the language they have been learning to use. Therefore, it is possible to 'invent' answers, or to do the activity as if they were someone else.

4 ¿Cómo era?

This activity gives the students the opportunity to practise the use of the imperfect tense and to revise the language of personal descriptions from earlier in the course. This is another activity which can be exploited orally to begin with, using graded questions to suit the stage which the learners have attained. This could then be followed up with written activities, including matching definitions, opposites and more open-ended activities like defining in their own language.

		Así se dice

Así se dice

Review the uses of the imperfect tense with descriptions. Students can turn to Activity C in *Práctica*.

5

Production
Based on the description given, students describe their imaginary former teachers.

6 *Y ahora tú*

Students now produce their own descriptions of people from the past.

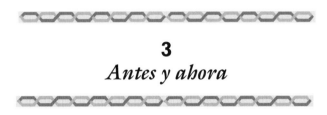

3
Antes y ahora

1

Input/Listening
After playing the recording through in its entirety, play through the first section in which Miguel talks about the present. Get the students to list the activities mentioned and the time on a grid. Depending on the students, you may wish to list the activities and times they take place. Students can then match them both, before putting them in sequence.

When this has been done for the current activities, do the same for activities in Spain and use the results as a basis for comparing both routines.

Así se dice

Read over the uses of **ahora** and **antes** and elicit from the students further examples of use.

2

Read the interview to the students before they look at it themselves, pausing and repeating sections to enable students to find a word or expression to fit in with the aspects of life compared in the following grid.

When this has been done, students can work on formulating statements about the past and present on the **estancia**. At this point they should be encouraged to use the written text, if necessary, for support.

	antes	ahora
1 horario		
2 almuerzo		
3 ventiladores		
4 heladeras		
5 agua		
6 campo		

3

Listening practice
List the key elements about the **barrio** and get the students to listen for the words used to describe them and to note them down as they listen to the recording.

Students could then be asked to imagine that Antonia's **barrio** had been the complete opposite and write an appropriate description to show this.

Así se dice

Read over the explanation of **hace X años** and **había**. Then return to the text of the recording to highlight examples of use.

4

Speaking practice
Students can take turns at asking each other: **¿Qué hay de raro/extraño en esta foto?** and at answering the question following the model given.

5 *Y ahora tú*

Using the model developed in Activity 3, get the students to put together a description of their home now, and then of a previous home. Once more, it is worth pointing out to the students that this need not be based on real life and might even be done in the persona of a film star or imaginary lottery winner.

▲▲▲▲▲▲ Temas ▲▲▲▲▲▲
En la pampa argentina

Los gauchos

Read the passage with the students and then ask them the following true/false statements.

1 **Pampas** is the name of the capital of central Argentina.
2 **Gauchos** was the name given to wealthy ranchers.
3 Argentina became independent from Spain in 1816.
4 The **ley de vagancia** was aimed at making the **pampas** a safe place for the **gauchos**.

5 The **gauchos** were arrested by the frontier patrols.
6 The native Indians were the enemies of the **gauchos**.
7 The fencing-in of the land made life easier for the Indians.
8 By 1870, Argentina had become fully industrialized.
9 The **gauchos** ended up working in factories.

Correction of this activity will lead to discussion of some of the most interesting points covered in the passage and should provide the opportunity for further exploration of the themes mentioned.

El último gaucho

Read the sections of the epic poem, **Martín Fierro**, to the students. Explore the first section in some detail, inviting the students to think about the tone of the poem and the emotions involved.

Next, get the students to work together in groups on providing a suitable English translation of the poem, which conveys the sense of loss, regret, frustration, etc.

Finally, get the students to work on readings of the poem which convey some, or all of the emotions. In particular, suggest that students concentrate on devising suitable patterns of intonation and stress, so that the key words and expressions are highlighted.

Veamos de nuevo
Gramática

Imperfect tense

This should confirm the students' hypotheses and extend what they have learned from the specific language encountered to the wider, more general context of all the verbs with which they are familiar.

■ Práctica

A

In this exercise, students are required to transform the information in the passage from first to third person. Use the exercise, not simply to change person, but also to ask a series of graded questions based on the content.

B Antes y ahora

To help reinforce the imperfect tense, get the students to complete the sentences with a verb in the imperfect tense.

C

Ask the students to make up a description of the man acting suspiciously. This can then be followed up by giving each student a picture of a different person – these can be simple 'paste-ups' of pictures from magazines. Students then have to work on building a description of the person in their picture.

When they have prepared the description, display all the pictures and each student takes it in turn to describe his/her suspect. The others have to select that suspect from the 'identity parade'. They can ask for supplementary information from the person composing the description.

■ Un paso más

1 Querida Claudia
Production
This activity requires students to distinguish between the imperfect tense and the preterite and is a useful supplementary activity for some students. As further practice/revision of the preterite tense, it may be helpful to ask students doing this activity to transform the preterite verbs from first to third person.

2 La mujer de ayer y hoy

Get the students to take turns at reading sections of the passage. In order to exploit the linguistic material in the passage, prepare the kinds of graded activities which have been done previously: matching words and definitions; finding synonyms/antonyms; true/false statements; giving further examples of the exercise in the student's book; choosing the correct statement from a series of alternative statements; correcting wrong information; and answering target questions.

3 El ganadero de Trujillo
Listening practice
This exercise is particularly challenging and so should only be attempted with the most able students. In addition to the usual pre-listening preparation, you will need to include a transcript of the key phrases and do substantial work on the background to the **trashumancia** – possibly by giving the students one of the many TV programmes/videos to view, before the first listening.

4 Checklist

Go through the checklist of activities with the students pointing out the new language from the unit and highlighting examples of use. On the whole, these should be elicited from the students, rather than proffered by you.

Unidad 14 *Las estaciones y el tiempo*

Functions

- Talking about the weather
- Making comparisons
- Saying which is the longest or the most expensive

Grammar

- Weather expressions
- Comparatives

Vocabulary

- Seasons
- Geographical locations
- Adjectives

Revision

- Months of the year

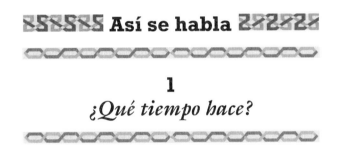

Así se habla

1
¿Qué tiempo hace?

1 Las estaciones

Input

Use OHT/Flashcards 14.1 to do a graded presentation of the seasons. This involves pointing to the pictures and inviting the students to:

1 repeat, chorally, at first, then individually: **Es la primavera/verano...**
2 identify whether a picture being pointed to, or held up, matches the Spanish name given: **Es el otoño, ¿Sí o no?**
3 select the correct name from two alternatives for the picture: **¿Es el otoño o el verano?**
4 correct wrong information: **¿Es la primavera?** (show **el invierno**)
5 answer a target question: **¿Qué estación del año es?**

Revision

Revise the months of the year. This can be done by writing the date on the board/OHP and asking: **¿Y el mes pasado, cómo se llama?** followed by **¿Y el mes**

que viene? then **¿Y el primer mes del año?** until you have covered all the months of the year and have written them on the board/OHP. You can then ask a few students to recite them, before removing some of them and asking other students to recite, filling in the gaps. By stages, you remove all the months of the year and the students should be able to recite them with some confidence.

Listening/Consolidation

Now play the recording and get the students to write down the months which are mentioned (or tick them off on a list/miniature calendar, if writing seems too difficult). Then go back and replay the recording and correct the activity with the group by asking questions in Spanish.

Note: As with all correction, try, where possible to avoid simply tallying scores and giving answers in English. Rather, take advantage to give the students further listening and speaking practice – this may be all they get from one week to the next.

2

Listening practice

Take each section of the recording separately. It may be useful to revise where each country is before listening to the recording and to read through and comment on the vocabulary list in the central panel: 'What word in English is similar to **época**?' '**Llover** and **lluvia** have the same root; **llover** is a radical-changing verb.' '**Seca** is used to mean dry in many contexts, as in English – **una persona seca**. How would you say a dry wine? ... a very dry wine? a very dry white wine?'

When this has been done, play the recording, but ask the students not to look at their books just yet. In correcting the activity, get the students to volunteer as much information as possible. If need be, ask graded questions in Spanish to elicit information about the seasons.

Así se dice

Consolidation

Review the new language which is listed here and take advantage to elicit from students the meanings and structure of **hay** and the fact that it is both singular and plural.

Go beyond the material on the recording and ask about the seasons in **la zona templada** and extend the situation beyond **la zona tropical** to areas within the experience of the students, such as: **¿Cuándo es el invierno en Londres? ¿Cuándo es el verano en**

Moscú? ¿Cuáles son los meses de la primavera en Nueva York? ¿Cómo es el verano en las islas Canarias? ¿Seco o lluvioso?

3 Y ahora tú

Production

Students can now work in groups to put together a short description of their country. In classes where students are all from the same area, it may be useful to give them an additional task of taking on the persona of a famous person and describing the climate in the country where that person lives/is from.

Take advantage of the opportunity to recycle language by getting the students to introduce themselves, say where they are from, where they live, etc. and then go on to talk about the climate.

4 El tiempo

Using OHT/Flashcards 14.2 depicting the various forms of weather, do a graded presentation. As in the course book, take care to keep the different kinds of structures separate to begin with and mix them freely after the graded presentation has been done.

It is extremely important, as with all graded presentations of new language, to elicit the pattern/ regularities from the students and not to give them abstract rules. Get them to tell you that some weather expressions use **hace** and others use **está** or **hay**.

5

Listening practice

Play the recording. Give the students the grid below and get them to record the weather mentioned.

	Estaciones	Tipo de clima	Tiempo que hace
Ecuador			
España			

Así se dice

Consolidation

Review the weather expressions and clarify the use of the present continuous (**está lloviendo/nevando**) as opposed to the present indicative (**llueve/nieva**). This does not usually present problems for English-speaking learners since the structures and uses are so similar in both languages. Draw the students' attention to **está nublado/despejado** and once more draw parallels with English.

6

Production

Using the map of Argentina, get the students to work out the weather in each of the regions mentioned. This

exercise can be used as the basis of pairwork to begin with, in which students take it in turns to ask: **¿Qué tiempo hace en…?** and pick a place on the map. Correct the exercise with the whole class, remembering that it is necessary to ask easier (graded) questions to weaker students.

Note: If a student makes a mistake, it can be more productive to move on to a student who can provide the correct answer and then return a little later to that student with the same or a similar question, than to embarrass the student by relentlessly insisting on the correct answer.

7

Reading practice

Read the passages describing the weather in three different regions of Spain, one at a time. Get the students to take turns at reading the passage. Use mainly alternative questions followed by target questions to interrogate the students about the content of each passage, for example: **El clima de Extremadura ¿es suave o es extremado?** followed by **¿Cómo es el clima de Extremadura?** This needs to be done at quite a brisk pace to give the students an opportunity to practise, without having time to get bored.

When you have exploited the passage orally/aurally, get the students to answer the questions set in the book.

8 Y ahora tú

Students can now work out a description of the weather on the particular day when they are working on this unit. This question should become part of the general pool of language which is frequently recycled throughout the remainder of the course.

2
En la costa el clima es más suave

1

Input

Before playing the recording, give the students the following grid and ask them to speculate about the meaning of the different elements of climate which are listed. They might be able to guess where each feature might occur.

While it is important to stress to students that they do not have to understand every single word they hear, it is also important to encourage them to try to make informed guesses about meanings they do not know and to look for patterns in structure. You should therefore suggest to them that they should try and work out the meaning of **más**.

Ciudades/Pueblos de la costa	Invierno	Verano
Lleida		
Pirineos		
Girona		
Tarragona		
más suave, más continental, más seco, más seca, más duro, más extremo, llueve más, llueve bastante poco, bastante frío, mucho calor, para ver nieve		

When the students have heard the recording several times, with pauses to enable them to fill in the grid, ask them to answer the questions in English, which follow the passage in the book.

Así se dice

Now read over the explanation of the comparative and refer back to the passage to illustrate and to give further examples.

2
Practice
Students have now got the language to be able to compare places on the map of Argentina on page 149. This should be done in writing first and corrected orally.

3 Y ahora tú

Students can now describe their own country, following the model used in Activity 3 in the previous section. If necessary, they can be given an outline map of the country, perhaps with major cities and weather symbols superimposed, to assist them in structuring the comparison.

Así se acostumbra

Read over the account of contrasting climates and landscapes within the Spanish-speaking world. It may be helpful to contextualize this information by having a wall map of the world so that students can see clearly where each place referred to is situated and to give them a sense of the enormous distances involved. Take advantage of having the wall map to revise geographical terminology and directions, such as: **¿Dónde está...?** **¿Cómo se llama el río más grande de Brasil?**

4
Listening practice
Get the students to make a table showing **campo**, **ciudad** and 'reason' along the top and numbers 1–3

down the side. Then play the recording through one example at a time and get the students to identify which is preferred, **campo** or **ciudad**. On the second and subsequent hearings of each example, get the students to identify the reason why. It is not important to understand the full explanation, as long as they get the gist.

5 Y ahora tú
Practice
Get the students to compare the cities using appropriate adjectives. Remember, there will be two comparisons for each pair of cities.

6
Practice
Students look at the characters in the illustration and answer the questions. When they have done this, they can do further practice in pairs. One student names two of the characters in the illustration and the other has to compare them using an appropriate adjective.

3
El río más largo del mundo

1 La más bella del mundo
Input
Read through the sentences and the names. Then get the students to match them up. In correcting the exercise, get the students to join them together using: **Es el/la...** Elicit from the student the meaning of **el/la más...**

2
Listening practice
Play the recording. It is not important to get all the information which is mentioned, but to find that which is asked for.

Así se dice

Read over the explanation of the formation of the superlative in Spanish. At the same time, get the students to suggest further examples.

3 Y ahora tú

Students could practise asking each other the three questions before writing down the answers.

4 La más bonita

Students may find this activity particularly taxing, because of the presence of unfamiliar vocabulary. It is therefore important to reassure them that the aim of the activity is to give them practice in identifying the key phrases which they need to answer the questions. For this reason, they should concentrate on identifying the language which is central to answering the questions.

5

Practice

Students refer back to Section 2, Activity 6 and use as many examples of the superlative to describe the characters in the illustration.

> ### Así se dice

Input

Revise briefly **gustar**, using flashcards or an OHT of, for example, tourist facilities. After briefly surveying attitudes to the various facilities, read over the explanation of the use of the superlative when expressing likes. You can then go back to the tourist facilities which have just been revised and ask: **¿Qué te gusta más?**

6 Y ahora tú

Production

Get the students to write out their answers to the questions about their preferences and take advantage to circulate and check spellings, use of accents, etc.

Temas
La tierra es frágil

La ruta verde

Read over with the students the account of the establishment and purpose of the green networks.

Paisaje tropical

Read the short story with the students. Then get them to categorize the vocabulary which is used according to both grammatical and situational criteria:

- Underline all the verbs in the passage.
- Underline all the words which refer to nature.
- List all the names for artificial substances.
- Underline all the words which have to do with boats.
- Underline all the adjectives.

When this has been done, get the students to do some of the following activities based on the above:

- Transform the passage from present to past tense.
- Define one of the sets of words.
- Match another set with a list of pre-prepared definitions.
- Summarize the story, using the key phrases from the existing one.

Destruccíon del medio ambiente

Read the passage on the state of the eco-system in Latin America with the students. Students could then make a table showing the problem in each country. This can be followed by composing statements in Spanish describing the main danger for each country. So, for example, if they have Brasil in one column and **la selva amazónica** in the next, they could write: **En Brasil, la selva amazónica está desapareciendo.**

España gráfica

Using the table at the foot of page 155, students can compare regions of Spain. This can be done orally through a series of questions which encourage/require the use of comparatives and superlatives.

Begin with a simple true/false type activity, based on a variety of statements, such as: **En Castilla-León el aire está contaminado. ¿Sí o no?** This can be followed by alternative statements, from which the students choose the correct one: **En Baleares ¿hay contaminación del suelo o del agua?** Next, incorrect information is given and the students have to correct it: **En Bilbao solo el agua está contaminada.** Finally, straightforward questions are asked: **¿Qué contaminación ambiental hay en Extremadura?**

Production

Students could now be asked to write something about the impact of pollution on the environment in their own country/city.

Veamos de nuevo
Gramática

1 Talking about the weather

Review with the students the expressions for talking about the weather.

2 Está nevando

Review with the students the use of the present continuous to emphasize action in the immediate present, not simply relating to weather, but to all areas of activity.

3 Making comparisons

Review thoroughly the comparative in Spanish. Emphasize the four irregular forms of the comparative adjective.

▪ Práctica

The exercises here are ideal for homework and can be corrected in class by you.

A Las estaciones

Ask the students to fill in the gaps with an appropriate word from the list. In correcting the exercise, avoid simply asking for the one word answer. Rather, ask questions which will require fuller answers and extension questions, such as the months which make up a particular season.

B Compara

This exercise gives further practice in the use of the comparative. Further work can extend from this activity if students are asked to give explanations for prioritizing one hotel over another: **El hotel Mar es mejor porque tiene más habitaciones.**

C Charlando

To give further practice in use of the present continuous tense, students should be asked to complete this exercise by putting the appropriate halves of the conversation together.

▪ Un paso más

1 La vela es más sencilla

Further practice of comparisons is provided in this exercise. It can be extended by getting the students to conduct mini-surveys within the class to establish what the distribution of preferences is within the class. This information can then be analyzed and communicated back, in Spanish, to the whole class.

2 Zonas húmedas de la Mancha

Reading practice/Production

Get the students to read over the descriptions of two routes. For more advanced students, you might even ask them to translate one of the passages. This can be followed by a series of true/false statements which the students identify correctly and some dictionary work on the definition of some of the 'technical terms' in the passage.

3 El tiempo

Listening practice

This activity should be prepared before listening to the recording. This can be done by the students making predictions about the kind of weather which is likely to be announced, on the basis of the symbols on the map. It could be corrected by giving the students a copy of the transcript after the activity has been completed.

4 Checklist

Go over the checklist of functions, situations and structures which students have learned in this unit. As each one is mentioned, elicit from the students several examples to illustrate it.

Unidad 15 *Pasó hace mucho tiempo*

Functions

- Telling your life story
- Saying how long ago and how long for
- Talking about history

Grammar

- Historic preterite, impersonal **se** + verb
- Personal **a**
- Object pronouns
- Irregular preterites: **hace, desde hace, llevar, conocer**

Revision

- Compass points
- Preterite
- Physical appearance
- Dates, numbers and time

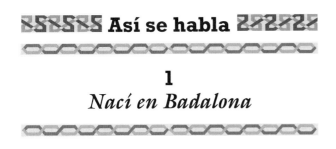

Así se habla

1
Nací en Badalona

1

Revision
Before introducing the use of the preterite tense through Mario Posla's account of his life, revise the names of countries where Spanish is spoken and their geographical location (**norte, sur, este, oeste**) using the map on OHT 1.1.

Listening/Input
Play the recording. Stop after each country is mentioned and get the students to match the expressions with the places. Then, correct the exercise in Spanish using graded questions, if necessary, to assist with meaning: **¿Nació en Estados Unidos o en Uruguay?** When the oral/aural stage has been completed, get the students to write out the statements in full.

Consolidation
Read over the explanations for the use of the preterite and go through the examples given.

Practice
To give further practice in the use of this structure, get the students to work in pairs completing the information-gap activity on Worksheet 15.1.

2

Reading/Speaking practice
Ask the suggested questions which follow the personal details. When this has been done, get the students to work in pairs and to take turns at being one of the Spanish architects and the interviewer. They can then go through the categories of information on the forms asking appropriate questions to elicit the required information: **¿Cómo se llama? ¿Dónde nació? ¿Qué estudió?** Review the use and construction of the preterite tense in Spanish by looking at Activity 1 in *Gramática*.

3

Listening practice
Before listening to one of the architects talking about his life, review the key elements in the life of both architects. Then, play the recording and ask the students to decide who is being spoken about. As with all practice, the main aim is not necessarily to be correct, but rather to practise using the target structures. Therefore, correction should require the students not simply to say who the person being described is, but also to explain why it is that person. Answers should be something like: **Me parece que es Jordi Moliner, porque nació en Badalona.** Students can then look at Activity C in *Práctica*.

4

Reading practice
Read over with the students the passage about Isabel Allende and the true/false statements on it. Stress that it is not necessary for them to understand every word, but that they should be looking for key information. You can then explore what this information might be and what linguistic clues they might look for, as well as clarifying the meaning of the statements.

In going over the passage for the second time, get the students to take turns at reading.

Many more statements, of the type which appear in the course book, can be made, time permitting. Moreover, you should move on to asking more difficult questions, such as alternative statements from which students choose the correct one, wrong information which students have to correct and target questions: **¿Quién? ¿Qué? ¿Cuándo?**

5 *De periodista*

Production

Students return to Activity 1 to write an account of Mario Posla's life. Prepare the activity orally with the whole class, before asking the students to write it up.

6

Production

Before tackling the task set, revise the vocabulary for describing physical appearance. Students can then complete the task, using the third person singular form of the verbs.

7 *Y ahora tú*

Production

Students use the first person singular to describe their personal details. If, for any reason you feel that this is a sensitive area, students can be given an outline of the details of a famous person and asked to 'play the part'.

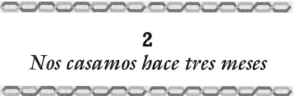

2
Nos casamos hace tres meses

1

Listening/Input

Before playing the recording, read over the questions in English and get students to make a list of language which might appear in the answers and which they already know. Take each interview separately.

2

Listening practice

Read over the questions to be asked before playing the recording. Then get the students to suggest what language they should be listening for in the interview, which will guide them to the answers. Play the recording, stopping and repeating sections, in order to give the students time to identify the necessary linguistic clues and information.

You might also ask the students to listen, on the second or third hearing of the recording, for any additional information they can pick up about María Elena.

3 *¡Una boda comentada!*

Reading practice

Prepare the questions in advance. Correct the activity, grading the questions to assist the weaker students.

4

Speaking/Writing practice

Students work in groups with the article to identify the main details of the account of the wedding. They then put the details together in a report which they read to the rest of the class.

5 *Y ahora tú*

Production

Students prepare the answers to the questions and then work in pairs, taking it in turn to ask and answer the questions listed. They can then report the answers they obtain to a wider group, or to the class as a whole.

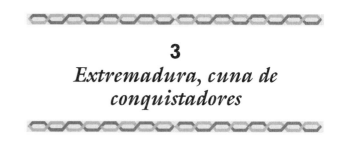

3
Extremadura, cuna de conquistadores

1

Reading/Input

Read over the statements which point the students to the key information they need to look out for in the passage.

For this activity, you will need a map of Spain and a more detailed, enlarged map of Extremadura so that students can follow the initial geographical description.

Make up further graded activities based on the passage, such as true/false statements and alternatives from which students have to choose the correct statement. You can then ask some target questions, such as: **¿Qué hay en el centro de la plaza mayor de Trujillo? ¿Cuándo reconquistaron los cristianos a Trujillo?**

2

Listening practice

Students listen for the names of places mentioned on the recording and plot these on the map. When correcting this activity, take advantage to revise the cardinal numbers: **el primero, el segundo...**

Así se dice

Consolidation

Revise the use of reflexive verbs in the preterite tense to refer to single historical moments.

3

Listening/Input

Revise the key information about historical dates, figures and names. Play the recording and get the students to listen and tick the names they hear.

Así se dice

Consolidation

Review the uses of the preterite tense in the examples given. Elicit from the students some of the important differences in use between the imperfect tense and the preterite tense. These examples provide a useful opportunity to contrast the tenses.

4

Production/Listening

Play the recording from Activity 3 again and ask a series of questions about each of the key people mentioned: **¿Cómo se llamaba? ¿Qué hacía? ¿Cuándo nació? ¿Cuándo murió? ¿De dónde era?**

5 Y ahora tú

Production

Invite the students to give the names of famous historical people and then to give brief details of the kind provided in Activity 3.

Practice

Students work in pairs or in small groups. Each student takes it in turn to pick a card from the pile of eight. The other student(s) then ask questions, using the preterite, about the identity of the person on the card. They ask as many questions as they like until they guess the identity.

ᐃᐃᐃᐃᐃ Temas ᐃᐃᐃᐃᐃ

De Extremadura salieron

Cortés en Méjico/Pizarro en el Perú

Read over the passages about Cortés and Pizarro and then get students to identify which of the following statements is true and which is false:

1 Cortés nació en Medellín en 1504.
2 Cortés fue a México porque necesitaba el dinero.
3 La mujer de Moctezuma se llamaba Malinche.
4 Cortés era buena persona.
5 En 1528, Pizarro fue a Panamá.
6 En 1532, Pizarro conoció a Atahualpa en Cajamarca.
7 Atahualpa quería ser amigo de Pizarro.
8 Pizarro murió en España.

Use the correction of the activity to discuss some of the issues arising from the Spanish conquest of Latin America.

Maldición de Malinche

Read the poem to the class and then get the students, working in pairs or small groups, to prepare a translation of one of the verses. This is a good opportunity to introduce the students to the notion that translation does not simply involve a word for word transfer, but is much more to do with conveying concepts.

In this way, students could produce translations of the poem which focus, not so much on conveying the literal translation, as on producing a faithful rendering of the poet's feelings.

⯀⯀⯀ Veamos de nuevo ⯀⯀⯀

Gramática

1 More about the past

This section reviews the use and construction of the preterite tense in Spanish and then focuses on the three irregular verbs: **venir**, **morir**, **tener**.

2 How long ago

Read over the explanation of the structure for using **hace** to say how long ago something happened and ask the students to make up some examples of their own.

3 How long for

In order to clarify for the students the use of **llevar**, read over the explanation given here. Several additional examples might be elicited from the students to illustrate use. This can be done by asking appropriate questions, such as: **¿Cuánto tiempo llevas en este colegio?**

4 Conocer

Read over with the students the explanation for the use of **conocer**, together with the need for the personal **a**. As with all new items of vocabulary, it is helpful if you give several additional examples – oral and in writing – and then elicit further examples from the students.

5 Him or Her

Read over the guidance for the formation and use of the personal pronoun.

6 Se construyó

Use of the impersonal form of the verb is clarified here. Explain to students what is meant by the passive and elicit several examples from them, in English, to reinforce their understanding. Only then will the impersonal **se** form make any sense to them.

■ Práctica

A Historia de dos ciudades

Read over with the students the passage outlining the history of the two Cartagenas. Students are given the infinitive forms of the verb and have to create the appropriate form of the preterite, using the guidelines they have just encountered above.

Depending on the amount of time available, you could then move on to exploit the passage further. This can be done by jumbling the order of sentences and getting the students to put them back in the correct order, without the assistance of the original passage.

B ¿Hace cuánto tiempo ...?

Students need to draw conclusions from the statements which are made as to the length of time which has elapsed since a particular event took place. It is worth ensuring, in English, that the students have understood the nature of the task, before asking them to go beyond the first one, which is a model.

C A busy day

This activity gives further practice in the use of the preterite tense first person singular. Get the students to prepare, in writing, the account given here. This will give you the opportunity to circulate and monitor students' writing skills.

■ Un paso más

1 ¿Conoces la historia?

Read over the historical events mentioned in this section and check that students understand them. Then get the students, individually or in pairs, to match up the events with the appropriate dates. It may also be necessary to revise dates in Spanish before students embark on this activity.

Subsequently, students can write out an account of the events by joining up the two columns to make complete sentences: **En 711, los musulmanes invadieron España.**

2 Pilar Miró

Students need practice in asking, as well as answering, questions. Before asking the students to write out the solutions for Task a), go over the exercise orally with the whole group.

Task b) provides further practice in talking about how long it has been since something happened.

3 The article

Production
Students read the article about Pilar Miró and prepare questions based on it. They then move on to preparing a report using all the information they have obtained.

4 Checklist

Go through the checklist with the students, eliciting from them a variety of ways of realizing the functions outlined.

Unidad 16 *¡A comer!*

Functions

- Ordering food in a restaurant
- Saying what you eat every day
- Describing recipes

Grammar

- Infinitive/Imperative
- Impersonal form with **se**
- Exclamations

Vocabulary

- **hace**

Revision

- Food and drink items

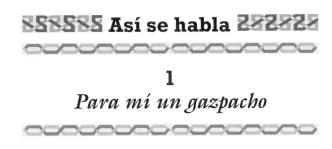

1
Para mí un gazpacho

1

Input

Use the illustrations of food from the menu on OHT/
Flashcards 16.1 and a graded presentation to present the
new language which the students will need for ordering
food in a restaurant. Revise the other menu items with
which students are familiar.

When the presentation and the revision have been done,
students work in groups to find the dishes listed.

2

Listening practice

Play the recording and get the students to fill in a menu
list like the one below to indicate each item ordered by
the customers.

	1	2	3	4
de entrada				
de segundo				
de postre				
bebida				

Remember to take the listening one customer at a time
and to give sufficient time for the students to hear and
note down the dish mentioned. This may mean
frequent replaying of each section. Students can get
further practice in Activity A of *Práctica*.

Así se acostumbra

Read over the passage on regional dishes with the
students and comment on elements of interest.
Students may well also be able to contribute from their
own experience and this should be encouraged.

3 *Y ahora tú*

Production

Using the framework of Activity 2, get the students to
take turns at asking for and taking orders of food, as per
the instructions. Before students begin working in pairs,
revise the questions which they might expect to be
asked or to ask.

4

Input/Listening

Tell the students they will hear people reacting with
pleasure to food. They have to decide what each
exclamation means and then tick it off in the dialogue
when they hear it. Play the recording so that the
exclamations are heard one at a time.

Así se dice

Consolidation

Read over the explanations of the significance of the
exclamations heard in the recording and confirm or
reject the students' predictions. Elicit from the students
the importance of adjectival agreement as well as some
additional examples to illustrate this. There are
examples of exclamations in Activity 3 of *Gramática*.

5 *Y ahora tú*

Production

Get the students to work on a role play, in pairs, as
waiter/waitress and customer. They should prepare a
dialogue based on the instructions given in the course
book. They should do this in stages: 1) arrival at the
restaurant with greetings, etc. 2) ordering food –
starters and main course, 3) commenting on the meal,
paying and leaving. Encourage them to improvize and
to incorporate language which they may have met
previously in the course.

6

Input/Listening

Use OHT/Flashcards 16.2 to introduce the desserts with a graded presentation. Then, play the recording and get them to tick each item of food on the menu, as they hear it mentioned.

> *Así se dice*

Consolidation

Go over the question forms, revising **hay** and **tiene**.

Practice

Give the students the information-gap activity about different flavours of ice cream on Worksheet 16.3. They then take turns at asking each other which flavours of ice cream they want. They answer according to the illustrations on the left, and fill in the answer from their partner on the right.

7 *Y ahora tú*

Production

Invite the students to work in pairs or in small groups preparing a role play, which involves selecting a dessert after enquiring what is available.

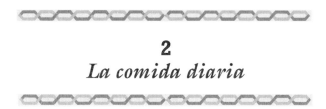

2
La comida diaria

1 *El desayuno*

Input

Present the breakfast items one by one – students have come across most of them before, and those that are new, are recognizable from cognates in English. Use a graded presentation to familiarize students with this area of language, but bear in mind that it is not necessary to go through all of the levels. For example, and this will very much depend on the stage of your learners, you could move from simple repetition to alternative questions and then to target questions.

> *Así se acostumbra*

Read through the account of breakfast habits in different parts of the Spanish-speaking world. Encourage students to talk about their experiences of eating habits in countries they have visited and to describe similarities with other areas of the world which they might have visited.

2

Listening practice

Revise food and drink items which might be consumed for breakfast. Play the recording. Get the students to indicate on the menu chart the items which are chosen and by which person. This can be done by writing EC for **ecuatoriano**, ME for **mexicano** or ESP for **español** beside each item of food/drink, as it is mentioned.

> *Así se dice*

Consolidation

Read over and comment on the explanation of how to ask about and describe the contents of meals.

3 *Y ahora tú*

Production

Based on the grid in Activity 2, organize the students to work in groups of about four or five. Using the 'round-robin' formula, each student takes it in turn to ask the person sitting to the right about his/her breakfast customs. They then report this information to the rest of the group, using the third person.

4 *La comida*

Listening practice

In order to assist understanding of the passage, give the students some key expressions in English and ask them to find the Spanish equivalent in the passage.

5

Listening practice

Play the recording. You could give the students a list of ingredients from which they have to select the ones mentioned. Alternatively, students could number each ingredient in the order in which it is mentioned.

> *Así se acostumbra*

Read over and comment on the information about **la comida rápida**. As on other occasions when customs are being described, it can be useful to explore similarities and differences between students' own experiences of food and those described here.

6

Listening practice

Play the recording. Students then tick the items off on a menu, or fill them in on a blank menu. Take advantage when correcting this exercise to give further practice by asking a series of graded questions in Spanish.

7 Y ahora tú

Production

In groups, students take it in turns to ask the person sitting on their right, one of the questions listed. They then report this information to the rest of the group. Alternatively, they can work in pairs, using the questions as the basis of an interview. When they have asked their partner all the questions, they can report the information gained to the rest of the class.

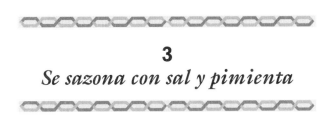

3
Se sazona con sal y pimienta

1

Input

Using OHT/Flashcards 16.4, do a graded presentation to introduce the verbs in this order:

1) **cortar, sazonar, picar, machacar, mezclar, calentar**;
2) **cocer, remover**; 3) **añadir, freír, batir**.

Use the illustrations and the **se** form of the verb for graded presentation:

Se sazona. (repetition)
¿Se sazona? ¿Sí o no?
¿Se sazona o se pica?
Se sazona. (False statement, as the illustration depicts se mezcla.)
¿Qué se hace?

Depending on the level of the students, you may not need to use all the levels of grading.

2

Practice

Students work in pairs and take it in turns to point to one of the illustrations of foods and to ask: **¿Qué se puede hacer?** Their partner gives the appropriate response using the impersonal **se**: **Se corta el tomate, se fríen las cebollas.**

3 Receta española

Listening practice

Play the recording and get the students to identify the ingredients in the recipe. If the students need more support, they could tick off the ingredients on a grid containing the names of all the foods.

4

Reading practice

In pairs, students should read over the jumbled recipe instructions and work out the correct sequence of actions.

Listening practice

In order to correct the activity, play the recording and get the students to match each step against their own answers.

> ### Así se dice

Consolidation

Read over the summary of the use of new structures. Concentrate on the plural form of the impersonal **se** and elicit from the students the fact that the plural form is used with a plural object.

5 Receta latinoamericana

Revision

Read over the recipe instructions for **guacamole**. Then, elicit from the students what is required to enable them to communicate the recipe orally to a friend, using the impersonal form. The first step is for the students to identify all the verbs which are in the infinitive and then to make the appropriate transformation.

6 Y ahora tú

Production

Students select their favourite recipes and describe them. Alternatively, you can give them a selection of recipes cut out of English magazines, from which to choose.

▲▲▲▲▲▲ Temas ▲▲▲▲▲▲
La comida es cultura

Los gustos de España

Read over the passage describing the characteristically Spanish ingredients and the way in which they were introduced to Spain. Do a brief oral translation of **Judías del tío Lucas**.

Hombres de maíz

This passage needs to be read over and commented on by you. Some students may have experience of other Latin American staple ingredients and these should also be discussed.

Las repúblicas bananeras

This passage, dealing with the importance of the banana for the economy of Central America, could be used as the basis of a true/false activity in which you compose a series of statements in Spanish. The students then have to decide whether the information given is true or not.

Read over the poem *Hora cero*, by Ernesto Cardenal. This can be used as the basis of a poetry reading by the students. Before the reading, however, it would be interesting to examine some of the key language. This can be done by means of a matching exercise in which translation equivalents are given in English and the students have to find the corresponding expressions in the text of the poem.

✖❮◆❯ Veamos de nuevo ◆❯✖
Gramática

1 Giving advice and instructions

Consolidation
Read over the summary of the structures used for giving instructions and advice. Pay particular attention to the radical-changing verbs.

2 Useful cooking terms

Explore with the students the use of prepositions in connection with food.

3 Exclamations

It can be profitable to take time to practise these examples of exclamations using simple flashcards with smiling/sad faces and a number of exclamation marks, as prompts, to indicate the degree of enthusiasm, or otherwise, which is implied: ¡–! ¡Qué pena! ¡+!
¡Qué bien! ¡¡++!! ¡Qué maravilla!

▪ *Práctica* ═══════════════

A Odd one out

This odd one out exercise is useful in giving the students some practice at handling the vast array of foods which appear on restaurant menus. Stress to the students that they are not required to understand every single word that appears in the lists. This therefore provides them with a good opportunity to learn/brush up on their dictionary skills. It is worthwhile taking time to go through with students the uses to which a bilingual dictionary can be put – i.e. it is not simply a question of finding the equivalent translation of a given term, but of finding the most suitable one from among a series of alternatives. It therefore requires a certain amount of thought and deduction to ensure that the most appropriate alternative is chosen.

This could also be a good opportunity to revise the alphabet which will assist the process of looking up words.

B ¡Qué .....!

This activity gives further practice in making deductions from statements where an exclamation is appropriate.

C En el restaurante

Before the role play, get the students to re-order and match up the questions and answers of the dialogue, between the waiter and his client.

D ¿Cómo se hace la sangría?

Students read over the ingredients and recipe for **sangría**. They could begin by identifying all the infinitives and giving, or finding, the English equivalent. They can then move on to identifying the ingredients. Finally, with the aid of a dictionary, they can translate the passage into English.

▪ *Un paso más* ═══════════════

1 What's in a dish?

Use the recipe to revise some of the new language which has been introduced in this unit. Give the students a list of expressions in English and get them to find the Spanish equivalent. Get the students to use a dictionary to find any words they don't know.

The end result could be a translation into English of the recipe. Students can then move on to describing their own favourite dish in Spanish.

2 ¿Dónde comemos?

Before doing this activity, get the students to describe – orally and then in writing – the tastes of the various members of the family, using **gustar**. Then, ask the students to make a list of what is available in each restaurant for each member of the family: **En El Pez Rojo mi marido puede comer...** Finally, they decide which establishment to use.

3 Todo con langostinos

Play the recording. Students identify three ways of serving prawns. Before listening, therefore, get the students to suggest different ways in which prawns might be served.

4 Checklist

Read over the checklist with the students and elicit from them suggestions for ways of carrying out the functions listed. This should include revising the new vocabulary, in particular new verbal structures, like the impersonal **se** form of the verb, weights and measures.

Unidad 17 *Sueños y deseos*

Functions

- Talking about your dreams and ambitions
- Giving instructions and commands
- Talking about what you like to wear

Grammar

- Imperative
- Imperative of reflexive verbs
- **llevar**

Vocabulary

- **hace, llevar**
- Clothing and preferences

Revision

- Likes and dislikes
- Descriptions, clothes and colours
- Professions

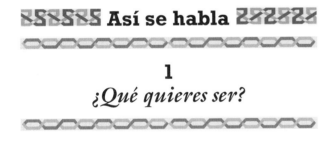

Así se habla

1
¿Qué quieres ser?

1

Listening/Revision

Focus on each illustration in turn and get the students to describe the people depicted. This is a good opportunity to revise the vocabulary for describing physical appearance as well as clothes and colours.

Input

Play, one at a time, the recordings of people talking about their dreams. After the first hearing, students should follow the dialogues in the book. When they have done this, ask a series of questions, graded, if necessary, about the content of each conversation, using the third person singular: **¿Qué quiere ser esta persona? ¿Quiere ser electricista? ¿Quiere ser electricista o mecánico?**

Review the ways of inquiring about and describing future plans. Elicit from students the fact that future wishes can be conveyed by combining the appropriate person of the verb **querer** with the infinitive of the verb or with **ser** + a noun depicting a profession.

2

Reading practice

Students match the sentences linking dreams and the people involved. Begin by clarifying the meanings of sentences 1–6. This can be done by asking appropriate questions, such as: **¿Quién quiere ser estudiante de medicina? ¿Qué es una abuela?**

When all the key words have been clarified in this manner, students can move on to matching up sentences 1–6 with statements a–f.

3

Listening practice

Play the full recording of the young woman talking about her dreams. Then get the students to identify her additional interests and ambitions. In correcting, take advantage to review the language encountered earlier.

4

Practice

In preparing this activity, it may be appropriate, depending on the level of the students, to offer alternative statements to the students for each of the illustrations. Their task is then to identify the statement which accurately describes the picture.

5 *Y ahora tú*

Practice

Get the students to work together in pairs, or in small groups, taking it in turn to ask each other about their dreams and plans for the future. This can be done using the 'round-robin' formula – one student asks a question of the person on his/her right and then reports the information gained to the rest of the group.

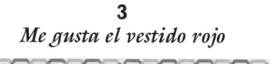

2
Sonría, por favor

1

Practice/Revision

Read over the pieces of dialogue with the class as a whole. Then ask the students to work in pairs linking each piece to the appropriate illustration. As preparation for this activity, it may be useful to explore the illustrations by asking questions about the appearance of the people depicted.

2

Input

Before doing this activity, revise the meanings of the verbs used in this section: **levantar, coger, beber, ir, venir, sonreír, acostarse, levantarse, sentarse**.

> ### *Así se dice*

Read over with the students the explanation of the use of the imperative. Put particular stress on the difference between formal and informal use of language and the need for appropriate use in context. See also Activity 1 in *Gramática*.

3

Elicit from the students the form of the verb which it is appropriate for a parent to use when addressing a child. Also review the way in which the imperative of verbs used in this activity is formed.

4

Practice

Further opportunity is provided here to practise the formal use of the imperative. Get the students to identify the verbs in the passage. When this has been done, establish the infinitive form of the verbs, in Spanish. You can then elicit from the students the correct form of the verb.

5 *Y ahora tú*

Production

Write a list of destinations on the board/OHP and ask students in turn to describe a suitable route. The others in the class can then guess the destination.

3
Me gusta el vestido rojo

1

Input

Use OHT/Flashcards 17.1 to introduce the articles of clothing by means of graded presentation. Begin with **sombrero/vestido**. Then move to **camisa, camiseta, chaqueta, falda** and **blusa**. Finally, introduce **pantalones, vaqueros** and **zapatos**.

Put a picture – head only – of a character on the board/OHP. Then, as you introduce each item of clothing, put it underneath the picture of the character. Begin with, **lleva sombrero**, which students repeat firstly in chorus and then individually. In presenting each item, follow the suggested order above, as this will help to focus students' attention on gender, thereby giving them categories to assist them in remembering the new vocabulary.

When you have introduced all the singular forms, in the repetition stage, move up through the grading in stages appropriate to the level of your students. This might mean, for example, asking alternative questions: **¿Y Juan, lleva camiseta o falda?** Then move on to asking target questions as you point at the article of clothing whose name you wish to elicit: **¿Qué lleva Juan?**

When all the items of clothing have been introduced, ask students to do the exercise in the book, matching illustrations of clothing with the appropriate word.

2

Listening practice

Before playing the recording, go over the list of vocabulary at the top of the central panel on page 185. Additionally, you should briefly revise the most common colours, by asking the colour of a variety of items in the room.

Elicit from the students the clues they might need to listen for in order to be able to identify the parts of the recording which are likely to refer to clothing: **Me pongo...**

Play the recording through once without interruption. Then, play each question and its corresponding answer, one at a time. It may be appropriate to give the students the support of the following grid and have them number each article of clothing in the order in which it is mentioned.

camisa de hombre	ropa negra
zapatos negros	camiseta
blue jeans	vestido oscuro
zapatillas blancas	pantalones cortos
vestido negro	blusa blanca
vieja camisa	sombrero

Así se dice

Review the expressions for asking about likes and dislikes and preferences. This is a convenient point to examine in more detail the variety of uses of **llevar** which can be done by looking at Activity 2 in *Gramática*.

3

Speaking practice

Students can work together asking: **¿Qué lleva?** and taking it in turns to point to an article of clothing which one of the models is wearing. This can be followed up by further pairwork, based on easily made prompt cards as described below.

From a mail order catalogue or magazine, cut out suitable pictures clearly depicting models wearing the articles of clothing which have been covered so far in this unit. Stick the pictures on to pieces of card and distribute one card to each student for use as stimulus material in pair- or groupwork.

Students do not show anyone else in their group the picture they have been given. Instead, the others take it in turns to ask a series of questions (graded if necessary) to elicit whether the model is male or female, old or young, etc. and what the model is wearing.

When this has been done, students could look at the picture and describe the colours of the clothes. In thinking about which clothes to mention, students could refer back to the list in Activity 2.

4

Listening practice

Play the recording, one speaker at a time. Repeat the recording of each speaker at least once more.

Remember, this is a practice activity and therefore correction should be done in Spanish, using graded questions where appropriate and avoiding the use of English, unless it is to clarify a specific point of grammar.

5 *Y ahora tú*

Production

In pairs, students take turns asking each other: **¿Qué llevas?** or **¿Qué ropa llevas?** When they have made a list of clothing, they can report this information back to the rest of the group.

Así se acostumbra

Read through the account of some examples of Latin American dress customs. This may lead to a more general discussion of the way in which traditional dress tends to be purely/mainly functional and thence to exploring other traditional dresses and their original purpose.

6

Listening practice

Play the recording and get the students to listen and to list the clothing in the order in which it is mentioned.

▲▲▲▲▲▲ Temas ▲▲▲▲▲▲

Las apariencias y las ilusiones

Sueños y pesadillas

Read the poem with the students. Examine some of the language by categories by asking students, for example, to identify and underline all the verbs. Orally, do a simple true/false exercise: **Quiere tener el pelo rubio como la muchacha. Le gusta el viento. Quiere estar cerca de la muchacha. Le gustan los pantalones cortos.** Students can answer, **sí/no/no se sabe.**

When this has been done, students can prepare a reading of the poem, concentrating on using appropriate stress and intonation to convey the feelings of the poet.

The next poem by Nicanor Parra can be used to practise talking about dreams. Elicit from students the difference between **soñar con** and **soñar que**. Students should be encouraged to make up their own poems using language which they already know/have encountered.

Diseñadores famosos

Read over the passage with the students and get them to identify which of the following statements are true and which are false:

1 Balenciaga is the Basque name for an evening dress.
2 Balenciaga lived in Paris for most of his life.
3 Balenciaga regarded himself as an artist rather than as a businessman.
4 No one ever saw Balenciaga in public.
5 Paco Rabanne was very different from his teacher in terms of personality.
6 Rabanne's designs were revolutionary.
7 The Spanish Infanta's wedding dress was designed by Rabanne.
8 Seville and Barcelona are the Spanish fashion capitals.

9 Caroline Herrera is Balenciaga's granddaughter.
10 Her designs are similar in style to Rabanne's.

La vestimenta también habla

This section can be read with the class as a whole and comments invited from students, particularly in relation to their own experience of Spanish-speaking countries or of their personal experience.

It is worthwhile drawing on similarities as well as on differences, since this encourages the notion, extremely important in foreign language learning, that other cultures are not completely different and that, where differences do exist, it is something to be respected as being of equal value. This parallels the psychological gap which students of a foreign language have to bridge in learning to accept that each language has a different, but equally valid way of describing reality and that no language is, in this respect, superior to others.

⬔⬔ Veamos de nuevo ⬔⬔
Gramática

1 Telling someone what to do

Read through and comment on the explanation of the use and form of the imperative. Give students a number of familiar, regular verbs and ask them to work out the correct form of the imperative.

2 Different meanings of llevar

Review all three uses of **llevar** with the students. In doing so, elicit further examples of use: **¿Cuántos años llevas estudiando español? ¿Qué ingredientes lleva la paella? ¿Qué ropa lleva...?**

3 Talking of dreams

Review the different ways of expressing dreams and ambitions. You may wish to discuss when it is more appropriate to use one expression in preference to another and to remind students of the differences between **quiero** and **quisiera**.

▪ Práctica

A Don't forget!

This exercise provides additional practice in the informal use of the imperative of regular **-ar** verbs. Initially, the exercise should be done orally/aurally with the whole class.

Subsequently, ask the students to write up the answers. Take advantage when the students are writing up the answers, to circulate and ensure that written work is accurate. Ensure that you pick up and correct errors sensitively. Additionally, you should make a mental note of mistakes, which can be highlighted subsequently, when correcting the exercise with the whole class.

▪ Un paso más

1 Day dreaming

Writing/Production
Get the students to compile an account of their own dreams and ambitions in accordance with the questions posed by the chat show host. This is a good opportunity to revise interrogatives and to ask students to give other examples of the use of **¿Quién? ¿Qué? ¿Dónde?**

2 Espartaco el torero

Reading
Students read over the interview and try to match up the information contained there with the list of statements placed before the reading.

Unidad 18 *De compras*

Functions

- Making plans and suggestions
- Buying clothes
- Buying souvenirs and bargaining

Grammar

- **ir a** + infinitive
- Order of pronouns before the verb
- Position of direct object pronouns

Vocabulary

- Times of day
- Future using **ir a** + infinitive

Revision

- Days of the week and months

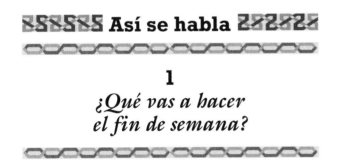

Así se habla

1
¿Qué vas a hacer el fin de semana?

Revision

Revise the days of the week. Use a calendar and, pointing to any date, ask: **¿Qué día es hoy?** When this has been done, revise the months too. Then practise **mañana**, **tarde** and **noche** with simple pictures of the moon/sun and a clock showing the appropriate times.

1

Input/Listening

Play the recording and then read over with the students the text and elicit from them the meaning of the infinitives: **hacer**, **comprar**, **venir**. Then ask them to identify the remaining verbs in the passage and to establish the infinitive of each one: **vas**, **necesito**, **quieres**, **puedo**, **tengo**, **estoy**.

Now play the recording a second time and establish which statements are true or false. As this activity will be done aurally/orally to begin with and then combined with reading, you could then move on to doing a more

exhaustive exploration of the passage in Spanish, using other levels of grading.

Así se dice

Consolidation

Now review the expressions for talking about plans and clarify the difference between **mañana** and **por la mañana**. This was covered already in the introductory unit at the beginning of the course.

2

Practice

After they have done the gap-fill/matching activity, correct the exercise with the whole class, taking time to elicit the patterns **por la...** and **...que viene**. Students can then move on to practising the dialogue by reading the part of Isabel or Maite. This can progress to a freer exercise in which they have to change three elements: 1) the days of the week, 2) the activity used as an excuse and 3) the time of day mentioned. For practice in **ir a** + infinitve, see *Gramática*.

3/4

Production

Students work together in pairs preparing the invitation for Maite and working out how to ask the right questions in order to ascertain the necessary information. They can then produce a small role play and take it in turns to be Maite and the person inviting her to coffee.

5

Practice

Now the students can practise using the third person singular to explain what Maite is going to do on Thursday and Sunday. Take advantage to elicit from students the key differences in the endings of the first, second and third person singular of the verb.

6 *Y ahora tú*

Use the questions as the basis of a role play pairwork between the students. They prepare the questions and answers and then rehearse the dialogue which they subsequently perform for the rest of the group.

Así se dice

Review ways of making and accepting/refusing an invitation to do something.

7

Listening practice

Play the recording and get the students to listen for key information in order to complete the table with details of the invitations and whether they are accepted or not. In correcting the activity, do not simply establish whether students have the correct answer or not. Rather, use the opportunity to give further oral/aural practice to the students, by asking the questions again in Spanish and eliciting answers in Spanish, which you then transpose on to a table on the OHP or board.

8 *Y ahora tú*

Production

A) Play the recordings and get the students to copy the model question, to produce an invitation to the other places mentioned.

B) Using the grid from Activity 7, get the students to identify the nature of the invitations left on the answerphone and, using the diary as a reference, to decide whether they are able to accept or not. Students can then practise using **no puedo**, together with **tengo que** + infinitive to make excuses.

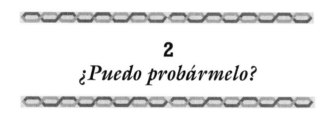

2
¿Puedo probármelo?

1 *Colores y diseños*

Input

Introduce the colours using flashcards of different coloured socks and a graded presentation. Begin with the colour on its own, in this order: **Es amarillo, rojo, blanco, negro** and **rosado**. This can be followed by **verde, azul** and **malva**, thus separating the adjectives which have gender and number agreement, from those which simply have number agreement.

When students are confident about identifying the base colours, introduce gradations: **azul marino, verde oliva**. Finally ask the question: **¿De qué color es?**

2 *En la tienda de ropa*

You will now want to introduce the notion of colours linked to adjectival agreement. This can be done by using the mail order pictures in the course book. First, ask questions about the garments depicted in the mail order excerpt. Then use the exercise as a paired practice activity in which the students take turns at pointing to an item and asking: **¿Qué desea?** to which the partner replies: **Quiero...** and names the item of clothing.

3

Listening practice

Depending on the level of the students, you could give them a list of possible items of clothing and colours and get them to number the relevant item and colour in the order in which they hear it mentioned. Alternatively, you could start by playing the recording and asking the students to write down the items they hear mentioned. Then, when you play it a second time, ask the students to identify the colours mentioned by each item. Correction should be done in the normal way by stopping the recording at the relevant section and replaying it so that students get practice at hearing the new language several times.

> ### *Así se dice*

Review the ways of asking for clothes in a shop and trying on garments.

4 *Quiero un vestido negro*

Practice

Based on the sequence of four cartoon frames, get the students to make up the dialogue which might be taking place. This exercise will need to be prepared orally, to begin with, before the students do any writing. Encourage the students to look for different ways of expressing the same idea. For example, rather than simply using **¿Lo tiene en azul?** you would accept **¿Lo hay en azul?** as a perfectly valid alternative.

5

Practice

Students should work together in pairs constructing short dialogues along the lines suggested in the book, varying the article of clothing and the colour.

6 *¿De qué material es?*

It isn't necessary for students to learn the names of all of the materials at this point, but it may be useful to identify key ones like **oro, plata, lana** and **algodón**.

Students can then work in pairs matching the articles mentioned in the lower frame with the materials in the upper one, using a dictionary where necessary to find out the meaning of new or unfamiliar words.

7

Listening practice

Students are listening for specific information here, and therefore they do not need to understand all of the conversation. Play each recording through once without pausing. Then move to playing, stopping and repeating the key information which will enable the students to fill in the grid with the relevant information.

8 Y ahora tú

Production

This section tests whether the students have in fact grasped the new language. It can therefore be used as an evaluation in which the task for the students is to work together in pairs to produce a role play. They should be encouraged to improvize and incorporate as much relevant language as possible, not simply from this unit, but from elsewhere in the course as well.

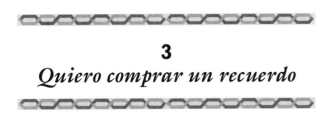

3
Quiero comprar un recuerdo

1

Read over this section and discuss the English names for items shown in the illustration.

Listening practice

Students are listening for clues to enable them to identify the souvenirs mentioned in San José and Cartagena. Students should have a table and insert items into each column accordingly.

Así se acostumbra

Read over and comment with the students on the **carreta**. Get the students to think about similar examples of souvenirs from elsewhere.

2

Listening

It might be useful to give the students a list of souvenirs to number in the order in which they hear them mentioned, since they will not yet have had sufficient practice to recognize all of them when they are embedded in a normal spoken text.

3 *El regateo*

Play the recording of the bartering in the market. Clarify the meaning of key words, such as **zampoña**. Ask students to identify and write down the numbers mentioned, in the order in which they are heard.

Así se dice

Read over the key expressions for bartering. Students could build a small role play along similar lines in which they take turns at being the stall holder and the customer.

Así se acostumbra

Read over the bartering tips provided. Students may wish to comment on the ethical issues involved or on the reasons why bartering is such an important feature of commerce in village and market life.

4 *Y ahora tú*

Production

This activity requires students to construct one side of a conversation in the market. It can be done in pairs, with one of the students playing the role of the stall holder. This can subsequently serve as a model for the construction of other dialogues around the purchase of different items in the market.

Temas
Manos juntas

La industria de las artesanías

Read the passage about craft industries and the influence of the multi-national corporations. In particular, read over and invite comment on the poem *Tarde o Temprano*. It may be appropriate to get the students to think about the point which the poet is making and to compose, as suggested in the book, a similar poem from their own experience.

Las arpillerías

The account of the origin of the **arpillería** is worth exploring in more depth. This is done by means of one woman's account of the composition of her first piece.

When the whole *Temas* section has been completed, give the students the bank of statements below to read and decide whether they agree (**estoy de acuerdo**) or disagree (**no estoy de acuerdo**) with what is being said, or are unsure (**depende**).

¿Cuál es tu opinión?

1 El efecto de las compañías multinacionales en el Tercer Mundo es malo.
2 Los pequeños negocios no sobreviven en el Tercer Mundo porque las materias primas son demasiado caras.
3 En realidad, no hay artesanía verdadera en ninguna parte.
4 Los turistas del mundo rico sostienen la artesanía en América Latina.
5 La cultura y las tradiciones son importantes. Es necesario mantenerlas.

6 Muchas de las tradiciones artesanales desaparecieron a causa de la influencia de los misioneros religiosos.

7 Las arpillerías son una forma de protesta pero no son el arte verdadero.

8 Las cooperativas son una forma de vivir alternativa a la sociedad moderna.

9 La experiencia de Mondragón puede funcionar en el resto del mundo.

10 La experiencia de Mondragón ha funcionado porque está en el País Vasco.

✕✕◆ Veamos de nuevo ◆✕✕

Gramática

1 Voy a visitar a mi madre

Read over with the students the explanation of the use of **ir a** + infinitive. It is important to draw their attention to the similarity between this structure and its English equivalent, which also uses 'to go to' + infinitive, to express future intention.

2 Me lo quedo

Read over the explanation of the direct object pronoun. Initially, it is not necessary to use the technical term, as this can often lead to confusion. Rather, concentrate on conveying the concept of what a direct object pronoun is and what function it fulfils. When students have grasped the concept, they will be ready to take on board the label.

Review the table of pronouns and then ask the students to supply the correct pronoun for familiar nouns. You could start with foodstuffs and then move on to clothing, etc.

3 Position of direct object pronouns

Read over this section and comment on the normal position of the direct object pronoun: before the verb. Then, look at the use of direct object pronouns when used with imperatives: after the verb, and with infinitives: either before or after the verb.

▪ Práctica

A Mil y una excusas

This gives the students some practice in making excuses and practising the use of the future with **ir a** + infinitive.

B Sí, lo compro

This combines the use of the correct pronoun in a meaningful exercise. Go over the first sentence with the students and then get them to use that as a model to do the remaining ones. Correct the activity with the class as a whole.

Then move on to get students to make up sentences combining the first person singular of **ir a** + infinitive with appropriate verbs, in accordance with the instructions given.

Así se acostumbra

Comment on the different systems for clothing sizes. This could provide a good opportunity for a brief revision of numbers: **¿Qué número en España es el 15 de Inglaterra?**

Review the use of the terms **talla**, **gasto**, **calzo**, **pequeña**, **mediana** and **grande**.

C ¿Qué talla usa?

This can constitute the basis of a brief activity in which the students ask each other about shoe size, clothes size, etc.

▪ Un paso más

1 Misahuallí Jungle Hotel

This exercise provides further practice in using the first person plural of **ir a** + infinitive to express future plans. Read over the itinerary first with the students and clarify the meaning of any language which is not understood. As at other times, use graded questions to elicit explanation/clarify meaning and avoid the unnecessary use of English: **¿Qué significa 'regreso'? ¿Significa 'volver' o significa 'llegar'?**

2 Compradores a la carta

Use the store guide as you would any text, as a rich source of language. Before embarking on the task set in the book, explore the rest of the guide by, for example, asking: **¿Qué se vende en el primer piso? ¿Dónde se pueden comprar...?**

3 Jarapas

Play the recording. Because of the level of difficulty of the language used by the shopkeeper in talking about Nijar's traditional crafts, it should be sufficient if students answer the questions in English.

Unidad 19 *¿Has visto la última película?*

Functions

- Saying what you have or haven't done
- Describing what has happened
- Recalling childhood memories

Grammar

- Perfect tense
- Irregular past participles

Vocabulary

- Entertainment
- Expressions of time
- Lost property

Revision

- Days of the week, time and months
- Pastimes

Así se habla

1
Esta semana no he hecho mucho

1

Input

Read over the introduction to the listening activity in order to set the context for the new language. Give out the chart of activities below and go over each one to ensure that the students understand them. Then play the recording and get the students to tick the chart to show which activities have been done by speaker A and which have been done by speaker B.

	A	B
1 hacer limpieza general		
2 dar un paseo		
3 ver videos		
4 tirar periódicos		
5 leer libros		
6 preparar ropa		
7 jugar al tenis		
8 ir al bar		
9 ir al cine		
10 hacer muchas cosas		

Consolidation/Listening

Play the recording in two stages. Firstly, play response A. When this has been repeated several times to enable students to grasp the new language, move on to response B. When this has been completed, return to the beginning of the recording and correct the exercise with the whole class.

Así se dice

Consolidation

Review the explanation/meanings of key phrases in this section before looking at a more detailed explanation of the use of the perfect tense. See also *Gramática*.

2 *¿Qué ha hecho Luis hoy?*

Reading practice

Read through the passage with the students and get them to identify/underline the infinitive forms of verbs. Then establish the third person form of **haber** and the past participles of the verbs in question.

3 *Y ahora tú*

Production

Students build their own responses to the questions. This can be the basis of a mock interview done with a partner, which is subsequently presented to the rest of the group.

4

Reading/Listening practice

Before listening to the recording, explain the meaning of **dicen que...** Then elicit from the students the title of the film which Luis and Carmen are planning to see and their expectations of it.

Así se dice

Review expressions for asking about experiences/activities using the perfect tense and its frequent combination with the preterite tense.

5

Production

Elicit from the students the names of some of the latest films currently showing in the cinema. Write these on the board together with three or four classics: **Sólo ante el peligro** (*High Noon*), **Lo que el viento se llevó** (*Gone with the Wind*), **Doce hombres sin piedad**

(*Twelve Angry Men*), **El último tango en París** (*The Last Tango in Paris*). Students then take it in turns to ask each other about which films they have seen and their opinion of it: **Es buena/mala.**

6 *Y ahora tú*

Production/Writing

Students prepare answers to questions. This could be followed up by **¿Cuándo?** and the preterite tense: **¿Cuándo estuviste en París?** Again, once the answers have been prepared, students take turns at rehearsing the mini-interviews as a pairwork activity and you select two or three pairs to perform the interview for the rest of the class.

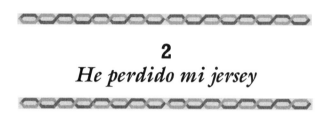

2
He perdido mi jersey

1

Input/Listening

Play the recording and then establish what has been lost, via a series of graded questions to avoid the need to go into English. **Y Jorge ¿ha perdido los zapatos?** should elicit the correct response: **No, ha perdido el jersey.**

If necessary, depending on the level of the students, give alternatives from which the students choose the correct answer, or simply accept a **sí** or **no** answer to questions. Questions should include **¿Dónde? ¿Cómo era? ¿Lo han encontrado?** and colours.

Así se dice

Review possible follow-up questions and answers.

2

Listening

Before playing the recording, review the questions to ensure that students understand the meanings.

3 *Y ahora tú*

Production

Get the students to put together a role play at the lost property office, using the items mentioned.

4 *En la comisaría*

Revision

Briefly revise physical descriptions and clothing before playing the recording. Then get students to compose a sketch of the characters involved. This can subsequently be corrected by the class as a whole.

5

Listening practice

This needs to be exploited in stages as with any other dialogue. Start by playing the recording and ensuring that the students have understood the gist of the passage. Then, move on to getting the students to take parts and read the dialogue. Next, remove key pieces of information and repeat the exercise, this time getting the students to fill the gaps with appropriate expressions.

This can be followed by the students doing the information-gap activity on Worksheet 19.1 in combination with the dialogue.

Así se dice

Review the expressions for reporting crime.

6

Firstly, using a dictionary where necessary to find the meaning of unfamiliar language, get the students to translate the names of the stolen objects. This activity can then serve as the basis of a more elaborate role play.

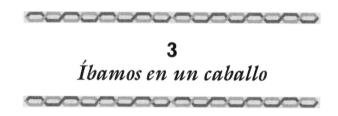

3
Íbamos en un caballo

1

Before reading the account of the events depicted in the illustrations, use these as the basis for exploring the language. Ask a whole range of questions, starting with simple questions about the village: **¿Cómo es el pueblo? Grande/pequeño, bonito/feo, abandonado/ concurrido. ¿Cuántos habitantes tiene – más o menos?** You can then move on to focusing the questions on the child: **Y el niño ¿cómo es? ¿Cuántos años tiene? ¿Qué ropa lleva?**

This kind of exhaustive exploration of visual stimuli is an extremely efficient way of revising language and preparing for a listening activity based on it. Most of it can be done using the present tense so that, even for the weaker students, the variables in terms of unknown language are kept to a minimum.

Listening practice

Play the recording and get the students to match up the accounts they hear and read with the appropriate illustration.

2

Reading

This passage needs preparation/revision of the names of relatives: **madre**, **padre**, **tío**, **tía**, **abuelo**, **abuela**. Do a true/false activity and then move on to answering the set questions.

3 *Y ahora tú*

Production

Students now put together a piece of writing about their own childhood memories. Depending on the level of the students, they will need more or less support, i.e. you may need to ask a whole series of graded questions to elicit responses which, when put together, will constitute a complete and continuous piece of writing.

Temas

La construcción del sueño

Antonio Gaudí

Read over the passage with the students and then get them to read the statements below and decide whether they are true or false.

1 Barcelona se fundó en el año 1880.
2 Entonces, muchas personas buscaban trabajo en Barcelona.
3 Antonio Gaudí es famoso por su arquitectura.
4 La arquitectura de Gaudí era moderna.
5 El estilo de Gaudí era artificial.
6 Le gustaban mucho las líneas rectas.
7 Gaudí tenía dos casas.
8 El Parc Guell está en Valencia.
9 La obra más famosa de Gaudí es La Sagrada Familia.
10 Gaudí murió de un ataque al corazón.

Recuerdos

Read the poem through with the students and then ask a series of general questions about it, such as: **¿De qué trata el poema? ¿Trata de una mujer o de una niña? ¿Cómo es la persona que habla? ¿Es joven o es mayor? ¿Cómo se sabe? ¿Qué ropa lleva?**

Similar questions can be asked in relation to each of the other two verses. Students can then put together six

sentences describing the poem and saying whether they like it or not.

Finally, get the students to prepare, in pairs, readings of one verse of the poem for performance to the rest of the class. As with other poetry readings, students should concentrate on using appropriate intonation and stress.

Veamos de nuevo

Gramática

1 Perfect tense

Review the structure of the perfect tense and the different persons of the verb **haber**. Examine the way in which the past participle is formed and draw students' attention to some of the most common irregular past participles. Remind them that this has already been encountered in Unit 11. Students could be asked to look up in the dictionary the meaning of the irregular past participles.

2 Expressions of time

Read over with the students this section containing a range of expressions of time which might occur in conjunction with the perfect tense. Subsequently, you might wish to ask the students to devise additional examples of their own using the same expressions of time.

Práctica

A Flash de noticias

Following on from the examination of how the perfect tense is formed, give the students practice in its use through this exercise. Firstly, students must identify the infinitive form of the verbs in the sentences and then form the appropriate past participle.

B ¿Qué tal te ha ido?

This transformation exercise requires the students to transform the verb from the infinitive to the perfect. It is important to get the students to translate the passage subsequently, so that the exercise does not remain purely mechanical.

C Mi maleta aún no ha llegado

This exercise provides additional practice in the use of the perfect tense, by requiring the students to match up two sides of a conversation.

1 *Joan Manuel Serrat*

The article about Serrat should be tackled by the students once they have done the work on the perfect tense. This does not require them to understand every word, but rather to look for the key information which is asked for in the book. This could be done orally to begin with – using graded questions to support understanding – or it could be a written activity to be done, with the aid of a dictionary, by students in need of additional work.

3 *¿Eres una persona aventurera?*

This exercise can be done either individually or in pairs, with students carrying out questionnaires with each other. Firstly, however, the students have to formulate the appropriate questions and this has to be corrected, before they embark on the survey.

4 *Checklist*

As in all units, the purpose of the checklist is to motivate the students by enabling them to see what they can actually do with the language they have learned. This should be done by eliciting from them examples of the functions outlined.

Unidad 20 *Te llamaré mañana*

Functions

- Talking on the phone
- Making arrangements to go out
- Talking about plans and intentions

Grammar

- Future tense
- Expressions of time

Vocabulary

- Phone language

Revision

- Greetings
- Time, days of the week
- Places in town

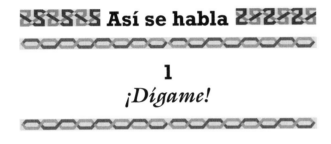

Así se habla

1
¡Dígame!

1
Input/Consolidation

Play the recording of the phone conversation once, without the students having the support of the written text. Then play it a second time with the students following the written text at the same time as they listen. Finally, get the students to match up the Spanish phrases with their English equivalents.

> ### Así se dice

Stress that it is not possible simply to translate English expressions used on the phone into Spanish on a word-for-word basis. Rather, it is necessary to use the conventions of each language. Indeed, it is worth pointing out that, even within the same language, different conventions apply from one country to another.

2
Practice

Play the recording of the phone conversations. Students fill in the gaps in the conversations and then rehearse the dialogues in pairs. When this has been done they can make up their own examples.

> ### Así se acostumbra

Review the variety of phone conventions across the Spanish-speaking world.

3
Listening

Play the recording one conversation at a time. It might be worthwhile asking students to predict what might be said. Elicit some of the key words or expressions.

4 *Y ahora tú*
Production

This should, at first, be done orally in pairs, with students changing roles and repeating the dialogue after the first round. Subsequently, they can write up the complete dialogue.

5 *Phoning the office*
Practice

In addition to listening for the key piece of information specified in the book – whether Lucía gets through or not – this dialogue provides a useful model for further dialogue practice along the same lines.

> ### Así se dice

Read through the range of possible replies the caller might encounter and invite the students to suggest contexts in which these might occur. Read over the explanation of the use of the indirect object pronoun **le** in *Gramática*.

6
Listening

This activity requires listening for key information. Students do not therefore need to understand every single word and some of the clues to meaning are not linguistic, for example the engaged tone.

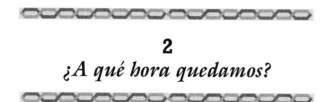

2
¿A qué hora quedamos?

1

Revision
Use OHT/Flashcards 20.1 to revise **la playa**, **el cine**, **de compras**. Then, use the smiling faces and unhappy faces as prompts to revise structures such as: **Me gustaría ir a la playa.**

Revise the 12-hour clock times and review the key language students might expect to hear when talking about meeting times. Then play the recording and get the students to fill in the information required.

| *Así se dice* |

Read over the various expressions for making suggestions and arrangements to meet. Then get students to practise the expressions using Worksheet 20.2.

2

Play the recording and get the students to fill in the grid with the key information. Although the introduction is very long, it does provide a good opportunity to recycle the language of greetings and, since the students will be reasonably familiar with it, they will be able to focus on the new language.

4 *Y ahora tú*

Get the students to work in pairs and build a dialogue/role play based on the invitation to lunch. To give them a clear model, it might be helpful – depending on their level – to put together a sample dialogue on the board/OHP, with suggestions from the class as a whole, before asking students to work in pairs.

| *Así se acostumbra* |

Read over the account of attitudes to punctuality in the Spanish-speaking world and explore with the students their own attitudes to punctuality. This should provide a good basis for deciding whether such attitudes form the basis of national characteristics/customs, or simply of stereotyping. You could move on from this issue to looking at other stereotypes which exist of Spanish speakers, such as Mexicans and Colombians.

5

Get the students to identify the habits of the speakers and their attitude to being on time.

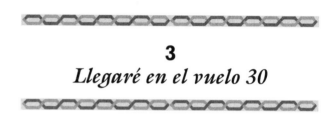

3
Llegaré en el vuelo 30

1

Read over the introduction and information which is asked for in relation to Luis's plans to stay with Isabel. Get the students to identify the verbs in the passage and elicit from them the meaning of the verbs. Then get the students to give further examples of use of these verbs, which they have previously encountered.

| *Así se dice* |

Review the expressions for talking about plans using the future tense.

2

Listening
Play the recording and get the students to number the list below to show which activities Isabel has organized for the weekend and in what order.

> **ir al teatro**
> **descansar**
> **ir a comer a casa de los Sánchez**
> **ir a comer con Pepe y Susana**
> **dar un paseo en el puerto**
> **venir la tía Berta**

Students can then write up the account in the third person plural, using the information from the list as a prompt: **El sábado irán a comer con Pepe y Susana.**

3 *Y ahora tú*
Production
Before attempting to compose a message for the answerphone, get the students to write a schedule containing the information outlined in the activity in the book. When this has been done, they can then use the information to put together the required message.

4 Buenos propósitos

Practice

Using the illustrations as prompts, the students work out Teresa's new year resolutions. Encourage students to use the expressions suggested in the book, such as **dejaré de** + infinitive.

Temas

Unidos en la lengua

"Cuento"

Read the excerpt from *Cuento* and invite the students to suggest what it is about. Then read over the passage and get the students to answer the multiple-choice questions below. When they have done this, go back and look again at the excerpt from *Cuento*, and ask the students whether they now understand the meaning better.

1 Aztlan

a) is a place in Mexico
b) was part of the Aztec empire
c) is an imaginary place
d) is too small to appear in the phone book.

2 Mexican Americans

a) became foreigners because of border changes
b) changed the names of cities in the USA
c) are a nomadic people
d) prefer seasonal work picking fruit.

3 The first Mexicans to arrive in the USA

a) arrived relatively recently
b) were part of existing communities
c) joined existing communities
d) arrived in the late 18th century.

4 The **espaldas mojadas**

a) is the Mexican name for the Río Grande
b) is the name of the Mexican immigrants to the USA
c) worked only as agricultural workers
d) were foreigners in Mexico.

5 The Hispanic population of the USA

a) is 13 million
b) lives mainly in Texas
c) comes mostly from Puerto Rico
d) is 22 million.

6 José Martí

a) was a member of Fidel Castro's army
b) lived in Florida
c) was Cuban
d) was the leader of the Cuban independence movement.

Hablando a voces

Read over the poems with the students. Then, ask them to select one of the poems and, working in pairs or small groups, to prepare a presentation for the rest of the group explaining the meaning of the poem for them: What is the tone? How does it change? What is the overall impression which the reader is left with? Finally, they can do a reading of the poem which they have worked on for the rest of the class.

Veamos de nuevo

Gramática

1 Talking about the future

Read over the explanation of the structure of the future tense and elicit from the students further examples. Read over the list of irregular verbs and elicit from the students suggestions for use.

Examine the use of the present tense to describe activities which take place in the near future.

▪ Práctica

A Cada loco con su tema

Read over the memo with the students and do the first example with the class as a whole. Then get the students to work on their own completing the rest of the exercise. When this has been done, go over the exercise with the whole group and do the corrections on the board/OHP, so that students see clearly what needs to be done.

B Madame Fifí

This activity is similar to the previous one, in that students have to practise putting the verbs in the future tense. Again, in order to establish the model for the class, do the first example with the class as a whole and, when the exercise has been completed, correct the exercise on the board/OHP.

▪ Un paso más

4 Tenerife

First of all, read through the brochure with the students and clarify, by means of graded questions, any language which they do not understand. Subsequently, get the students to underline all the verbal structures in the passage and to identify the infinitive form of the verbs in question. They should now be in a position to put the verbs in the future tense, as appropriate.

5 Checklist

As in previous units, go through the checklist with the students eliciting from them examples of the functions listed. It is important to be positive and encouraging and to emphasize how much students can actually do with the language, rather than getting bogged down in the complexities of grammatical structure.

Worksheets
OHTs/Flashcards

Hola ¿Qué tal? / Buenos días ¿Cómo está?

1		🙂
2		☹️
3		😐
4		☹️ ☹️
5		🙂 🙂

🙂 🙂	🙂	😐	☹️	☹️ ☹️
muy bien	bien	regular	mal	fatal

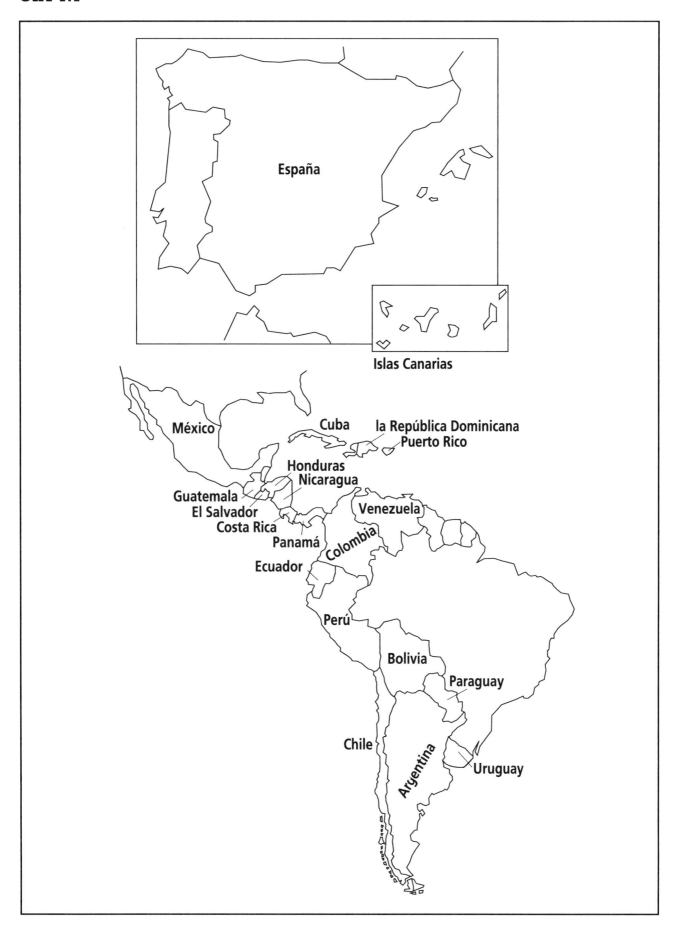

España

Islas Canarias

México

Cuba

la República Dominicana
Puerto Rico

Honduras
Nicaragua

Guatemala
El Salvador
Costa Rica

Venezuela

Panamá

Colombia

Ecuador

Perú

Bolivia

Paraguay

Chile

Argentina

Uruguay

Worksheet 1.2

A

Cuba

Honduras

Guatemala
El Salvador
Costa Rica

Colombia

Ecuador

Bolivia

Chile   Argentina

Worksheet 1.2

B

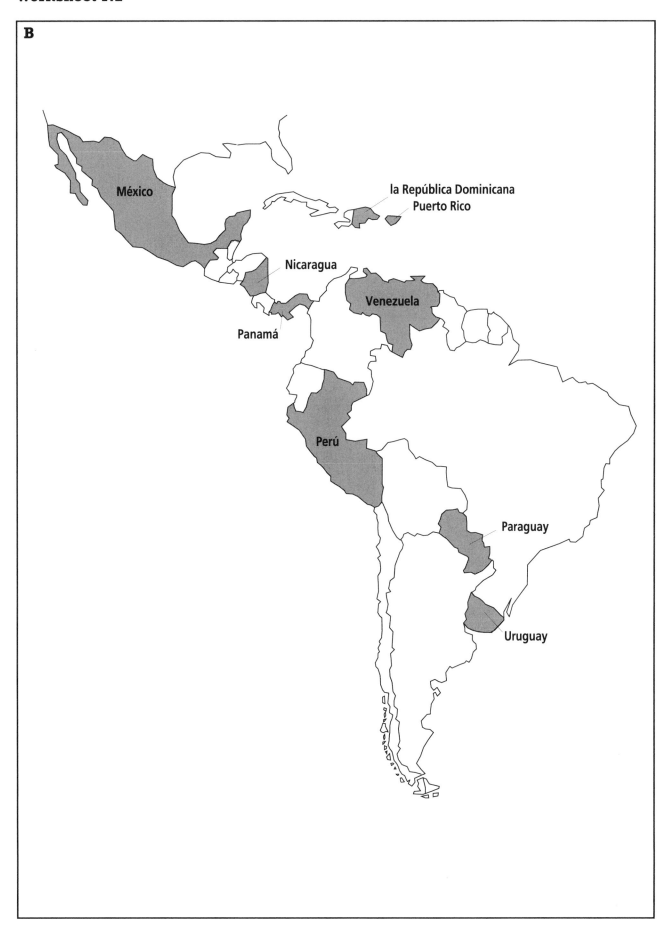

México

la República Dominicana
Puerto Rico

Nicaragua

Venezuela

Panamá

Perú

Paraguay

Uruguay

Worksheet 1.3

A	Nombre	Ciudad	País
1. María Florencia		Lima	....
2. Antonia Sánchez		Valparaíso	....
3.		....	....
4.		....	....

B	Nombre	Ciudad	País
1.		....	....
2.		....	....
3. Marco Antonio		Quito	....
4. Raquel Hernández		Salamanca	....

Worksheet 1.4

1   **El español: idioma mundial**

¿Verdad (✔) o mentira (✗)?

1. Spanish is spoken across the whole of the Iberian peninsula. .... ☐

2. In all the republics of Latin America, French, English, Dutch, Portuguese and
   many indigenous languages are spoken. .... ☐

3. In the U.S. there are around 17 million speakers of Spanish. .... ☐

4. 15th century Spanish is spoken in Israel. .... ☐

5. Apart from Spanish, two other languages are spoken in the Basque country in Spain. .... ☐

6. Only Spanish was permitted during the Franco dictatorship. .... ☐

7. Spanish is a comparatively new language in Latin America. .... ☐

8. The Aztecs were not a friendly people. .... ☐

9. Quechua is still a very important language in Latin America today. .... ☐

10. Several native languages are still spoken in Latin America today. .... ☐

11. Some of the commonest words in Europe today originated in the languages
    of the native inhabitants of Latin America. .... ☐

12. Spanish is one of the few European languages which has managed to remain
    uncontaminated by other cultures. .... ☐

Worksheet 1.4

2   **Ruben Blades: 'Salsero Social'**

Fill in the following form with details of Ruben Blades.

Surname ....   Name ....

City of residence ....   Age ....

Studies ....   Mother's occupation ....

Married/Single/Divorced ....   Ambition ....

3   Draw lines to match up the words and expressions from the song *Muévete* with their English equivalent.

1. **bala**   a. to kill

2. **acabar**   b. the children

3. **cantan**   c. bullet

4. **los niños**   d. evil

5. **matar**   e. they sing

6. **maldad**   f. to put an end to

7. **Canta**   g. people

8. **gente**   h. sing!

Worksheet 2.1

¿De qué nacionalidad es?						
	inglés/inglesa	francés/francesa	argentino/a	americano/a	africano/a	español(a)
Nelson Mandela						
Madonna						
Mitterand						
Maradona						
Plácido Domingo						
Montserrat Caballé						

Worksheet 2.3

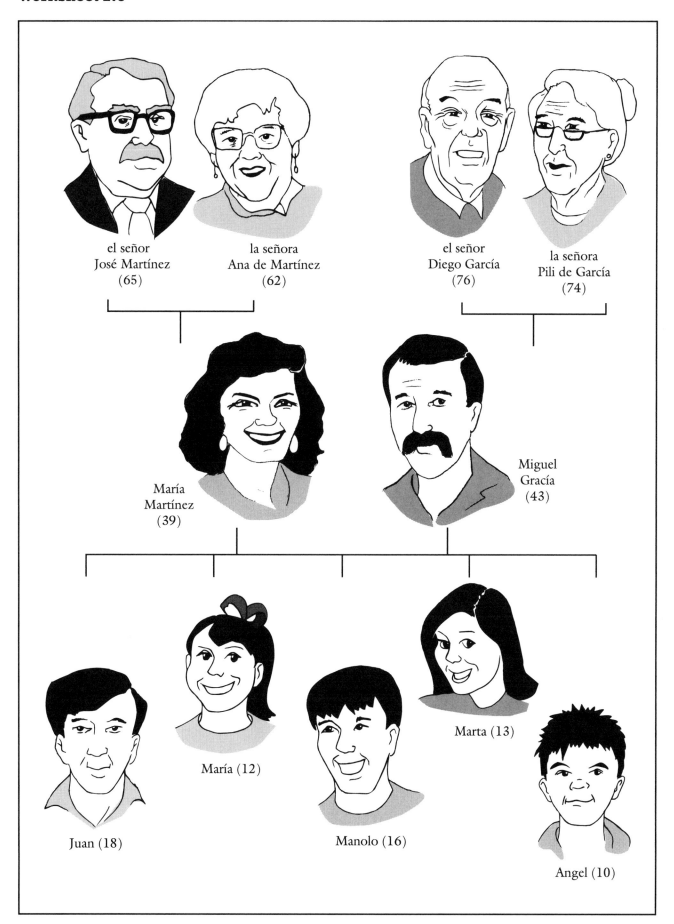

el señor
José Martínez
(65)

la señora
Ana de Martínez
(62)

el señor
Diego García
(76)

la señora
Pili de García
(74)

María
Martínez
(39)

Miguel
Gracía
(43)

Juan (18)

María (12)

Manolo (16)

Marta (13)

Angel (10)

Worksheet 3.1

A1	A2	B1	B2
Juan	....	....	Berta
Lima	....	....	Madrid
Barrio la Luz	....	....	Alcobendas

A3	A4	B3	B4
Oscar	....	....	Loreto
Montivideo	....	....	Santiago
Barrio San José	....	....	Barrio San Pedro

A5	A6	B5	B6
Adriana	....	....	Auxi
Buenos Aires	....	....	San Sebastian
Boedo	....	....	Itxurtzi

Worksheet 3.3

A	Santa Cruz	Elche	Miramar	Rosas	B	Santa Cruz	Elche	Miramar	Rosas
	2	....	4	....		....	15	....	X
	1	....	1	....		....	8	....	X
	4	....	7	....		....	20	....	X
	1	....	2	....		....	6	....	1
	2	....	3	....		....	12	....	X
	1	....	1	....		....	2	....	1
	3	....	6	....		....	9	....	1
	1	....	2	....		....	5	....	X

Worksheet 4.1

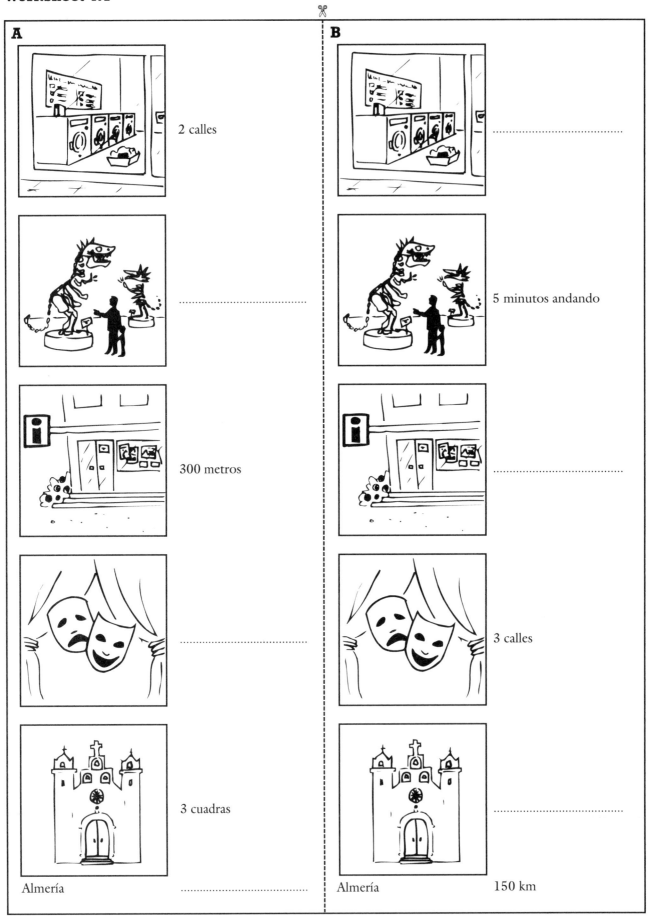

A

2 calles

300 metros

3 cuadras

Almería ....

B

....

5 minutos andando

....

3 calles

Almería   150 km

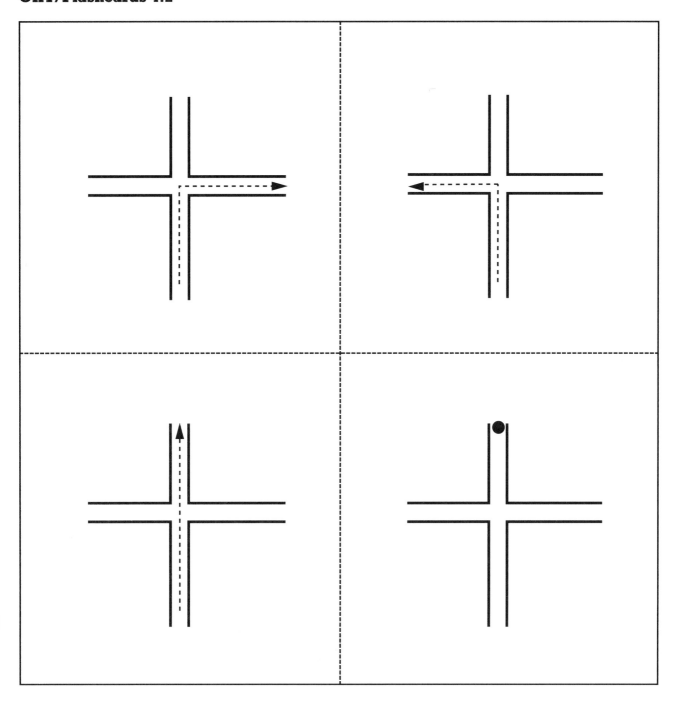

Worksheet 5.2

Take turns with your partner at being one of the customers below or the shop assistant.

A tick in the box means the customer asks for that item of groceries.
Remember to greet the shopkeeper/customer before dealing with the grocery list!

	Marco (quiero)	Claudia Patiño (quería)	Carlos Silva (quisiera)	Carmen Rosa (por favor)	Tú
		√		√	
	√		√	√	
		√	√		
	√			√	
	√	√	√		
				√	
	√				

50 gramos

100 gramos

$^1/_2$ kilo

1 kilo

1 $^1/_2$ kilos

1 L

Worksheet 5.4

A (1) Begoña	(2)	(3) Ramón	(4) ....
1 barra grande	....	2 barras pequeñas	....
2 kilos	....	3 kilos	....
200 gramos.....................	....	100 gramos	....
2 litros.....................................	....	1 litro	....

B (1)	(2) Ana	(3)	(4) Juan
....	2 barras pequeñas	....	3 barras grandes ....
....	4 kilos	....	1½ kilos ....
....	250 gramos	....	400 gramos ....
....	2 botellas	....	3 litros ....

Worksheet 5.5

Jaime es el carpintero del barrio. Hay tiendas nuevas en el barrio.
Help Jaime to match up the pictures of the shops with the correct names.

a. pastelería   b. confitería   c. panadería   d. frutería   e. charcutería   f. pescadería   g. carnicería

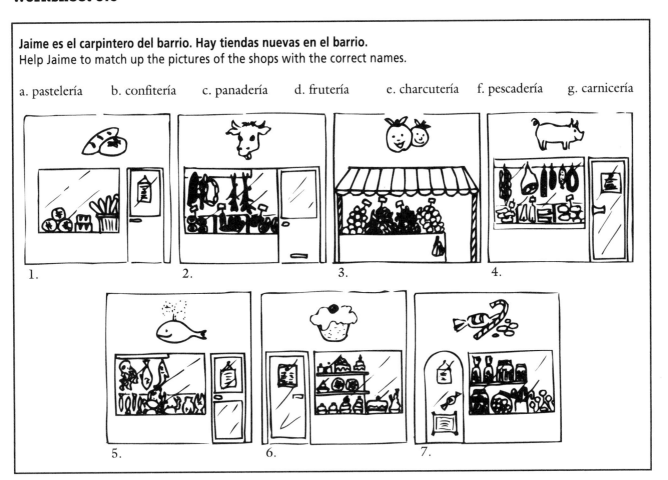

1.   2.   3.   4.

5.   6.   7.

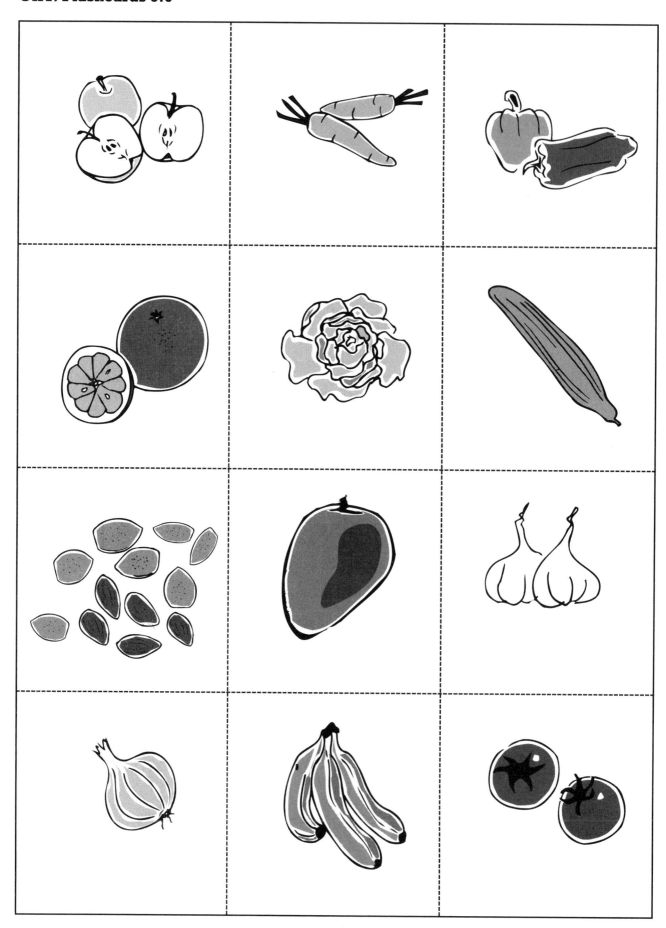

Worksheet 5.7

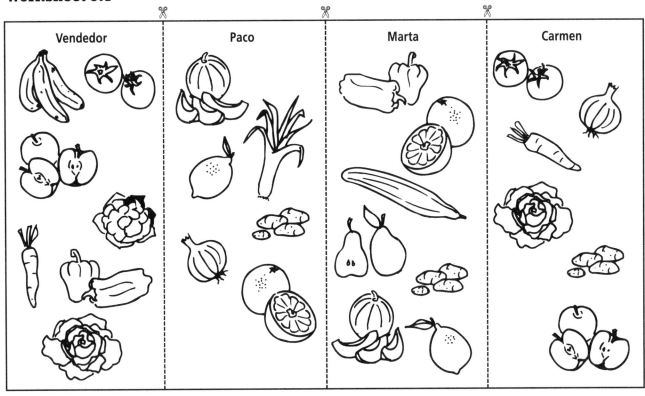

	Vendedor	Paco	Marta	Carmen

131 . **5**

OHT/Flashcards 6.1

OHT/Flashcards 6.2

Worksheet 6.3

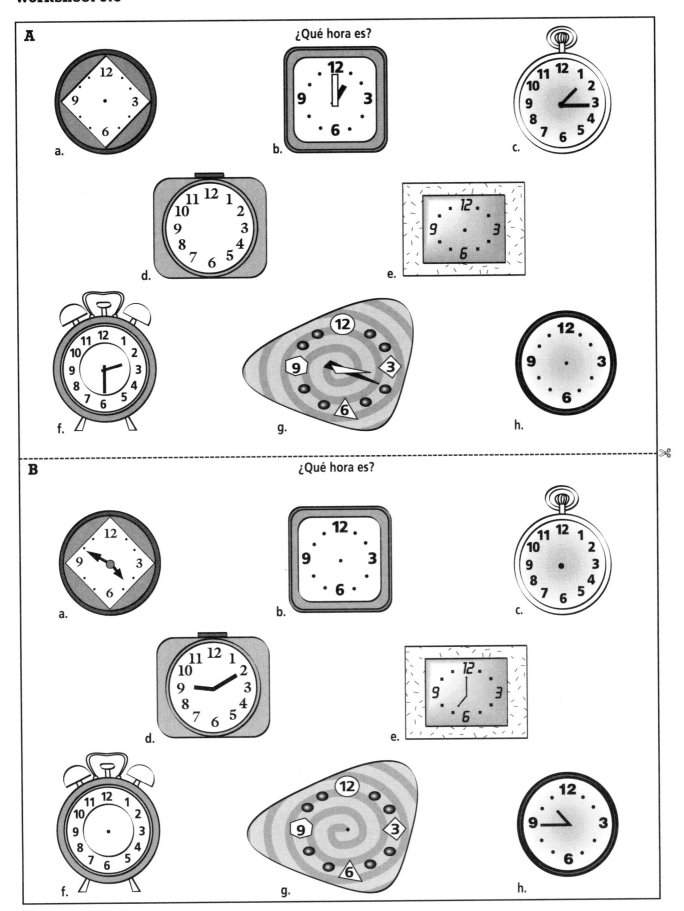

A

¿Qué hora es?

a.

b.

c.

d.

e.

f.

g.

h.

B

¿Qué hora es?

a.

b.

c.

d.

e.

f.

g.

h.

OHT/Flashcards 7.1

OHT/Flashcards 7.2

Worksheet 7.4

A	Le gustaría...	Me gustaría...

1. ....

2. ....

3. ....

4. ....

5. ....

B	Le gustaría...	Me gustaría...

1. ....

2. ....

3. ....

4. ....

5. ....

OHT/Flashcards 8.2

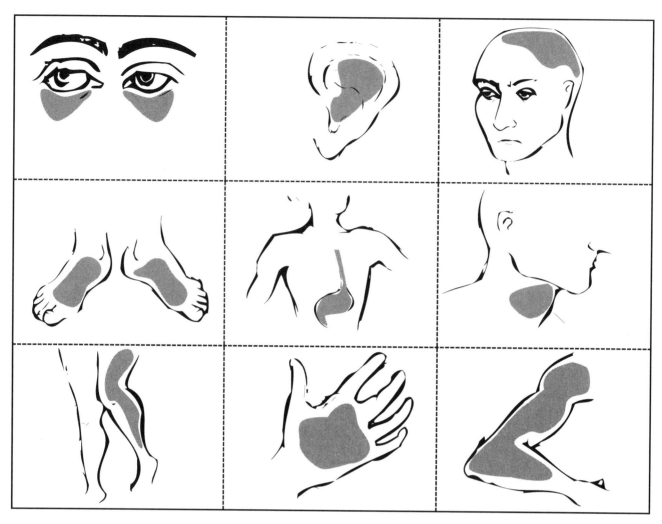

Worksheet 8.3

✂

A	¿Qué le sucede?	**B**	¿Qué le sucede?
1.	....	1.	....
2.	....	2.	....
3.	....	3.	....
4.	....	4.	....
5.	....	5.	....

138 . **8**

Worksheet 8.4

Describe these people.

a

b

c

d

e

f

139 . **8**

Worksheet 9.2

A — ¿Qué le gusta hacer?

♥ = le gusta ♥♥ = le encanta ♥̶ = no le gusta ♥♥̶ = no le gusta nada

	TV	paseo	cine	tiovivo	cama	libro
Juan						
Ana	♥	♥♥	♥♥̶	♥	♥̶	♥♥
Miguel						
María	♥♥	♥	♥♥	♥♥̶	♥̶	♥
Antonio						
Eva	♥♥̶	♥̶	♥	♥♥	♥♥	♥♥̶

B — ¿Qué le gusta hacer?

♥ = le gusta ♥♥ = le encanta ♥̶ = no le gusta ♥♥̶ = no le gusta nada

	TV	paseo	cine	tiovivo	cama	libro
Juan	♥	♥♥	♥	♥̶	♥♥̶	♥♥
Ana						
Miguel	♥♥̶	♥	♥̶	♥♥	♥	♥♥
María						
Antonio	♥♥	♥♥̶	♥♥	♥	♥♥	♥̶
Eva						

Worksheet 9.3

A		B	
a. 14/03	....	a.	03/01
b. 09/10	....	b.	27/11
c. 23/08	....	c.	08/09
d. 30/12	....	d.	13/04
e. 01/07	....	e.	24/02
f. 15/05	....	f.	19/06

OHT/Flashcards 9.4

OHT/Flashcards 10.1

Worksheet 10.2

A — ¿Qué medio de transporte usan normalmente?

	🚌	🚇	🚕	🚗	🚆	🚶	🚲	✈️
Juan	✔	✔				✔		
María								
Ana			✔	✔				✔
Antonio								
Miguel	✔			✔			✔	
Eva								

B — ¿Qué medio de transporte usan normalmente?

	🚌	🚇	🚕	🚗	🚆	🚶	🚲	✈️
Juan								
María		✔			✔	✔		
Ana								
Antonio		✔		✔				✔
Miguel								
Eva	✔		✔		✔		✔	

OHT/Flashcards 11.1

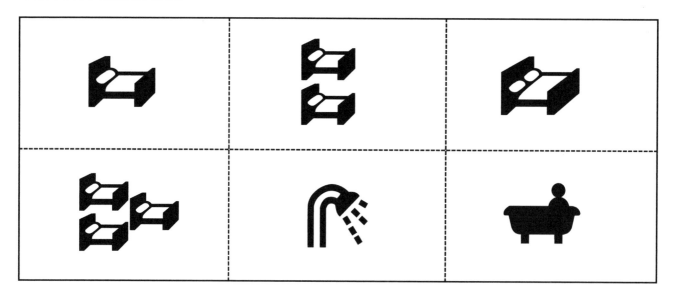

OHT/Flashcards 11.2

OHT/Flashcards 11.4

OHT/Flashcards 12.1

Worksheet 12.2

A	¿Adónde suele ir de vacaciones?					
	Viña del Mar	Acapulco	Marbella	Mallorca	San Juan	Ibiza
Carmen		✔				
Ion			✔			
Andrés				✔		
Priscila						
Anita						
Eva						

- ✂

B	¿Adónde suele ir de vacaciones?					
	Viña del Mar	Acapulco	Marbella	Mallorca	San Juan	Ibiza
Carmen						
Ion						
Andrés						
Priscila	✔					
Anita					✔	
Eva						✔

Worksheet 12.3

A1 — ¿Dónde fuiste de vacaciones?

Ciudad	Visitas	Compras	Comida	¿Qué tal?

❤ = me gustó   ❤❤ = me gustó mucho   ❤❤❤ = estuvo fenomenal

A2 — ¿Dónde fuiste de vacaciones?

Ciudad	Visitas	Compras	Comida	¿Qué tal?
Valencia	la catedral		paella	❤
Alicante	la Plaza de España/ el castillo	flores		❤❤❤

❤ = me gustó   ❤❤ = me gustó mucho   ❤❤❤ = estuvo fenomenal

A3 — ¿Dónde fuiste de vacaciones?

Ciudad	Visitas	Compras	Comida	¿Qué tal?

❤ = me gustó   ❤❤ = me gustó mucho   ❤❤❤ = estuvo fenomenal

A4 — ¿Dónde fuiste de vacaciones?

Ciudad	Visitas	Compras	Comida	¿Qué tal?
Buenos Aires	el barrio de Boedo/ el puerto	libros/guía	restaurante	❤❤❤
Punta del Este	la playa	sombrero	pescado	❤

❤ = me gustó   ❤❤ = me gustó mucho   ❤❤❤ = estuvo fenomenal

Worksheet 12.3

B1 — ¿Dónde fuiste de vacaciones?

Ciudad	Visitas	Compras	Comida	¿Qué tal?
Quito	el casco colonial/ Museo del Banco Central			♥
Cuenca	el río	joyas	tapas	♥♥

♥ = me gustó　　　♥♥ = me gustó mucho　　　♥♥♥ = estuvo fenomenal

B2 — ¿Dónde fuiste de vacaciones?

Ciudad	Visitas	Compras	Comida	¿Qué tal?

♥ = me gustó　　　♥♥ = me gustó mucho

B3 — ¿Dónde fuiste de vacaciones?

Ciudad	Visitas	Compras	Comida	¿Qué tal?
Granada	el Alcázar/ el Generalife	cerámica		♥♥
Córdoba	la Mezquita	chaqueta de piel	vino	♥♥♥

♥ = me gustó　　　♥♥ = me gustó mucho　　　♥♥♥ = estuvo fenomenal

B4 — ¿Dónde fuiste de vacaciones?

Ciudad	Visitas	Compras	Comida	¿Qué tal?

♥ = me gustó　　　♥♥ = me gustó mucho　　　♥♥♥ = estuvo fenomenal

Worksheet 12.4

A	¿Qué hiciste la semana pasada?			
	Ana	Jajana	Martín	María Elena
leer un libro	23:15	....	20:00	....
levantarme temprano	07:10	....	07:15	....
ir a la piscina	07:55	....	08:30	....
subir a la montaña	12:20	....	–	....
visitar a mis amigos	–	....	12:40	....
volver a casa	20:00	....	16:45	....

B	¿Qué hiciste la semana pasada?			
	Ana	Jajana	Martín	María Elena
leer un libro	....	07:00	....	21:35
levantarme temprano	....	06:30	....	06:50
ir a la piscina	....	08:25	....	–
subir a la montaña	....	–	....	14:40
visitar a mis amigos	....	14:35	....	16:30
volver a casa	....	15:40	....	20:00

OHT/Flashcards 14.1

OHT/Flashcards 14.2

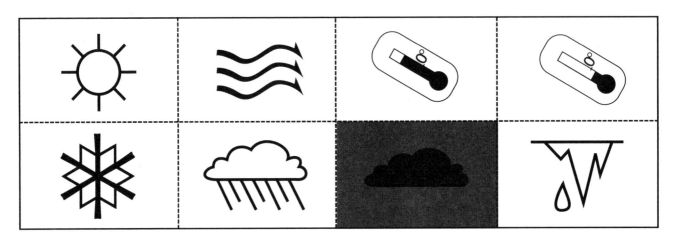

Worksheet 15.1

A

Nombre	Pablo Picasso	Mario Vargas-Llosa	Pablo Neruda	Isabel Allende
¿Dónde nació?	....	Arequipa (Perú)	....	Lima
¿Cuándo nació?	....	1936	....	1942
¿De niño, dónde vivió?	....	Bolivia	....	Santiago
¿Qué estudió?	....	letras	....	periodismo
¿Dónde trabajó?	....	París	....	Caracas

B

Nombre	Pablo Picasso	Mario Vargas-Llosa	Pablo Neruda	Isabel Allende
¿Dónde nació?	Málaga	....	Parral, Chile	....
¿Cuándo nació?	1881	....	1904	....
¿De niño, dónde vivió?	Galicia	....	Temuco	....
¿Qué estudió?	arte	....	francés	....
¿Dónde trabajó?	París	....	Santiago	....

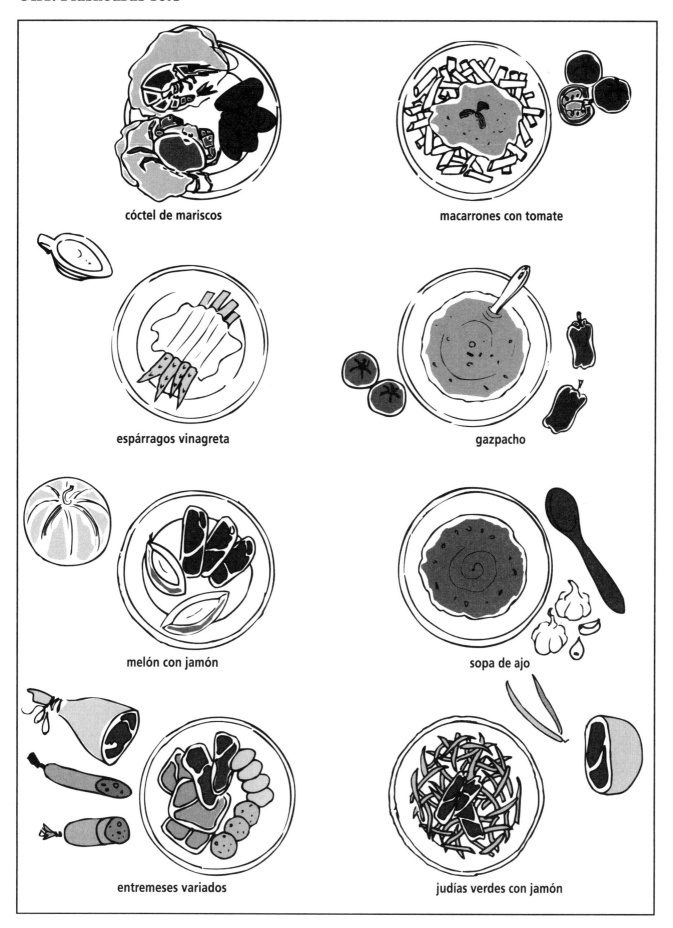

cóctel de mariscos

macarrones con tomate

espárragos vinagreta

gazpacho

melón con jamón

sopa de ajo

entremeses variados

judías verdes con jamón

OHT/Flashcards 16.2

Worksheet 16.3

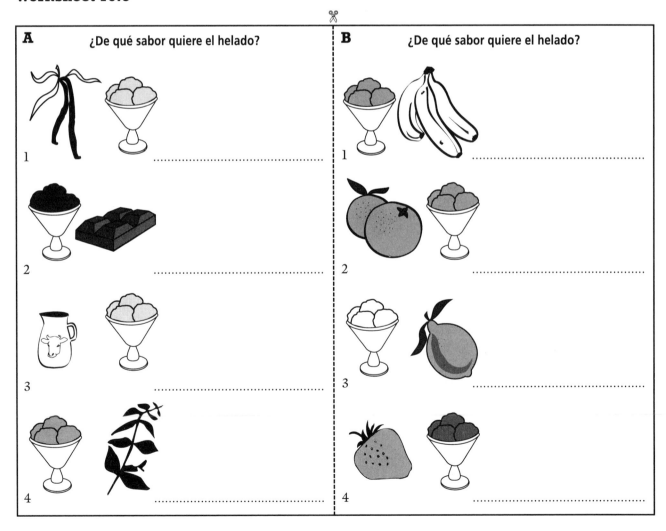

A — ¿De qué sabor quiere el helado?

1 ....

2 ....

3 ....

4 ....

B — ¿De qué sabor quiere el helado?

1 ....

2 ....

3 ....

4 ....

154 . **16**

Worksheet 19.1

La oficina de objetos perdidos				
A	**1**	**2**	**3**	**4**
Objeto robado	bicicleta	....	maleta	....
¿De qué color?	verde	....	marrón	....
¿Dónde?	la calle mayor	....	Paseo de la Habana	....
¿Quién?	chico	....	chica	....
¿Edad?	15 años	....	17 años	....
¿Cómo era(n)?	rubio, alto	....	pelo largo, castaño	....
¿Qué llevaba(n)?	pantalón vaquero	....	falda pantalón roja	....

✂

La oficina de objetos perdidos				
B	**1**	**2**	**3**	**4**
Objeto robado	....	coche	....	reloj
¿De qué color?	....	blanco	....	de oro
¿Dónde?	....	la Plaza de España	....	la playa
¿Quién?	....	hombre	....	chico
¿Edad?	....	25 años	....	19 años
¿Cómo era(n)?	....	moreno, pelo corto	....	rubio
¿Qué llevaba(n)?	....	pantalón gris camisa azul	....	pantalón corto

OHT/Flashcards 20.1

OHT/Flashcards 20.2

¿Quedamos?